Understanding Economic Forecasts

Understanding Economic Forecasts

edited by David F. Hendry and Neil R. Ericsson

The MIT Press
Cambridge, Massachusetts
London, England

Library of Congress Cataloging-in-Publication Data

Understanding economic forecasts / edited by David F. Hendry and
  Neil R. Ericsson.
    p. cm.
  Includes bibliographical references and index.
  ISBN 0-262-08304-3 (hc.: alk. paper)
1. Economic forecasting. I. Hendry, David F. II. Ericsson, Neil R.
HB3730 .U49 2001
330′.01′12-dc21   2001042740

To Evelyn and Karen

Contents

List of Figures   xi
List of Tables   xiv
Preface   xv
List of Contributors and Their Affiliations   xvii

1   **Editors' Introduction**   1
1.1   Economic Forecasting   2
1.2   An Analogy   4
1.3   Forecasting Methods   7
1.4   Evaluating Forecasts   9
1.5   Summary of the Chapters   10

2   **How Economists Forecast**   15
David F. Hendry
2.1   Introduction   15
2.2   Forecast Terminology   17
2.3   Some Essential Background   20
2.4   Methods of Forecasting   24
2.5   On Winning at Forecasting   26
2.6   On Determining the Forecast Winner   27
2.7   Forecast Confidence Intervals   27
2.8   How Economists Analyze Their Methods   29
2.9   The Main Problems Affecting Economic Forecasts   33
2.10   Forecasting 300 Years of UK Industrial Output   34
2.11   Some Potential Solutions   40
2.12   Conclusions   41

3   **Economic Modeling for Fun and Profit**   42
Paul Turner
3.1   Introduction   42
3.2   Alternative Forecasting Methods   44

3.3	A Basic Model of the UK Economy	47
3.4	Concluding Remarks	52

4 Making Sense of Published Economic Forecasts **54**
Diane Coyle

4.1	A Famous Forecasting Competition	54
4.2	Spurious Precision	57
4.3	Forecast Errors	59
4.4	Confusing Public-service Forecasts with Targets	62
4.5	Forecast Uncertainty and Policy Lags	63
4.6	Forecasting Is Difficult	65
4.7	Conclusions	66

5 Forecast Uncertainty in Economic Modeling **68**
Neil R. Ericsson

5.1	Introduction	68
5.2	Forecasts, Outcomes, and Forecast Errors	70
5.3	Sources of Forecast Uncertainty	76
5.4	Conclusions	91

6 Evaluation of Forecasts **93**
Clive W. J. Granger

6.1	Model Evaluation in Economics	93
6.2	Forecasting Background	95
6.3	Evaluation of a Point Forecast	97
6.4	Different Situations for Evaluation	99
6.5	Forecasts and Decisions	100
6.6	Concluding Remarks	103

7 Forecasting and the UK Business Cycle **104**
Denise R. Osborn, Marianne Sensier, and Paul W. Simpson

7.1	Introduction	104
7.2	The Nature of the UK Business Cycle	108
7.3	Univariate Business-cycle Models	110
7.4	Interest Rates and Output Forecasts	115
7.5	Measures of Forecast Accuracy	120
7.6	Concluding Remarks	122

8 Modeling and Forecasting at the Bank of England **124**
Neal Hatch

8.1	Introduction	124
8.2	Models, Forecasts, and Policy	125

8.3   A Suite of Models   138
8.4   Properties of the Bank's Core Model   142
8.5   Other Modeling Techniques and Information Sources   145
8.6   Conclusions   148

9   Forecasting the World Economy   **149**
Ray Barrell
9.1   Introduction   149
9.2   Endemic Structural Change   153
9.3   European Labor Markets   154
9.4   Japanese Consumers' Expenditure   156
9.5   The East Asian Financial Crisis, 1997–1998   157
9.6   The Collapse of LTCM in 1998   159
9.7   Living in a Low-inflation World   160
9.8   Inflation Uncertainty in the United Kingdom   164
9.9   Conclusions   169

10   The Costs of Forecast Errors   **170**
Terence Burns
10.1   Introduction   170
10.2   The General Case for Economic Forecasting   171
10.3   Some Characteristics of Forecast Errors   173
10.4   Forecast Errors Under a Given Policy Framework   175
10.5   Choosing the Policy Framework   181
10.6   Conclusions   183

11   Epilogue   **185**
David F. Hendry and Neil R. Ericsson
11.1   A Retrospective   186
11.2   A More Formal Approach   188
11.3   Concluding Remarks   190

References   **193**

Author Index   **203**

Subject Index   **205**

Figures

2.1 The effects of incorrect or changing deterministic terms   23

2.2 Which wins: forecasts of levels or growth?   28

2.3 Estimated densities of residuals from the model of UK narrow money   30

2.4 Forecasts from the model of UK M1 and forecasts of the artificial series, all with fans depicting forecast uncertainty   31

2.5 Densities of four estimated coefficients from the model of the artificial data   32

2.6 UK industrial output and its growth rate, 1715–1991   35

2.7 Densities of the growth and acceleration in UK industrial output, 1715–1825 and 1715–1991   37

2.8 Forecasts of UK industrial output over successive 50-year horizons   38

2.9 Zero-acceleration and constant-trend forecasts over 10-year horizons, 1801–1850   39

3.1 Disinflation with backward-looking and partly forward-looking expectations   50

3.2 Output cost of disinflation with backward-looking and partly forward-looking expectations   51

3.3 Disinflation paths with a Taylor interest-rate rule and a Friedman monetary rule   52

3.4 Output cost of disinflation with a Taylor interest-rate rule and a Friedman monetary rule   53

5.1 Forecasts, outcomes, and forecast errors of the US trade balance   71

5.2 The Bank of England's November 2000 fan chart for projections of RPIX inflation   72

5.3   The November 2000 projection by the Bank of England
      for the probability density of RPIX inflation in the year
      to 2002Q4   73
5.4   Four examples of possible histograms and estimated
      densities for forecast errors   74
5.5   Actual, fitted, and forecast values from the trend and
      random-walk models of annual real net national in-
      come for the United Kingdom   81
5.6   The US/UK exchange rate, and its monthly rate of
      change   84
5.7   Histograms and estimated densities of forecast errors
      for the US/UK exchange rate at various horizons   85
5.8   Histograms and estimated densities of one-month
      ahead forecast errors for the US/UK exchange rate
      over two subsamples   86
5.9   Hypothetical variances of forecast errors, as a function
      of the degree of persistence and of the forecast horizon   87
5.10 Actual and forecast values from two models of the real
      US trade balance   88

7.1   Output and interest rates over the UK business cycle   108
7.2   Output forecasts from univariate models and from
      models using interest-rate information   111
7.3   Regime-switching probabilities as functions of
      interest-rate changes   117

8.1   The Bank's forecast process   127
8.2   The August 1999 fan chart for the Bank's inflation fore-
      casts   130
8.3   The August 1999 fan chart for the Bank's GDP growth
      forecasts   131
8.4   The probability of inflation being within 0.05 percent-
      age point of any given inflation rate   133
8.5   The distribution of RPIX quarterly forecasts for 2001Q3   134
8.6   Mean RPIX inflation projections and outcomes from
      the *Inflation Report*   135
8.7   The ratio of house prices to earnings   136
8.8   The first two moments of annual RPIX inflation   137
8.9   Ratios of various inventory measures relative to GDP   139
8.10 Private sector earnings growth and settlements   140
8.11 Official data for, and survey-based estimates of, man-
      ufacturing output   141

8.12 Measures of consumer confidence 142

8.13 CBI business optimism and annual GDP growth 143

8.14 Influences on manufacturing investment 144

8.15 A schematic for the monetary transmission mechanism 145

8.16 News about monetary policy 146

8.17 The August 1999 projection for RPIX inflation based on market interest-rate expectations 147

9.1 The German unemployment rate 155

9.2 Swedish and Finnish unemployment rates 155

9.3 Residuals for the equation of Japanese consumers' expenditure 157

9.4 US unemployment and inflation rates 161

9.5 The US real effective exchange rate 161

9.6 Residuals for the US wage equation 162

9.7 95% confidence intervals for UK inflation under money-stock targeting and under a combined money-and-inflation rule 167

9.8 95% confidence intervals for UK inflation under a combined money-and-inflation rule and under an inflation-targeting rule 168

Tables

2.1   Means and standard deviations (in %) of Δy_t and $\Delta^2 y_t$ 36

3.1   Comparison of GDP forecasts from time-series and structural models (£1000 million at 1990 prices)   46

6.1   Values arising from different events and decisions, and forecast and subjective probabilities for the events   101

7.1   Forecast performance of the four empirical models   120

8.1   Other forecasters' expectations about RPIX inflation (probability, per cent)   135

Preface

The British Association for the Advancement of Science, or BAAS, exists to communicate scientific ideas and developments to non-specialists. The Economics group ("Section F") of the BAAS has a long and distinguished history of pursuing this goal for economics, with many of the United Kingdom's most famous economists having addressed Section F at some stage. Indeed, two of Section F's recent presidents—James Mirrlees and Amartya Sen—are Nobel Prize winners.

During September 15–16, 1999, the British Association held its Annual Festival of Science at the University of Sheffield, Sheffield, England. Presentations to Section F, under the presidency of David Hendry, focused exclusively on economic forecasting. After considerable revision and editing of the papers given, the present volume resulted.

We are indebted to members of Section F of the BAAS, particularly Peter Sinclair and Donald Anderson, for their support in bringing this publication to fruition, and to several anonymous referees for helpful comments and suggestions about the chapters herein. We are also grateful to Terry Vaughn (then at MIT Press) for encouraging us to produce this book, and to Elizabeth Murry for seeing it through to completion.

In addition, we wish to thank Anindya Banerjee, Gunnar Bårdsen, Julia Campos, Jurgen Doornik, Clive Granger, Eilev Jansen, Søren Johansen, Katarina Juselius, Hans-Martin Krolzig, Massimiliano Marcellino, Grayham Mizon, John Muellbauer, Bent Nielsen, Adrian Pagan, and Neil Shephard for their comments, discussions, and constructive criticisms. We are especially grateful to Jurgen Doornik for his help with the styles and computer setup for generating camera-ready copy, and for the use of his excellent OxEdit and indexing programs. Scientific Workplace (MacKichan Software, Inc., Bainbridge Island, Washington, USA), in combination with MiKTEX and DVIPS, eased the writing of the book in LATEX.

The views in this book are solely the responsibility of the authors and should not be interpreted as reflecting the views of the Board of Governors of the Federal Reserve System, or of any other person associated with the Federal Reserve System.

David F. Hendry and Neil R. Ericsson
Oxford and Washington, DC
August 2001

List of Contributors and Their Affiliations

Ray Barrell, rbarrell@niesr.ac.uk, National Institute of Economic and Social Research, London, UK.

Terence Burns, burnsunit@compuserve.com, House of Lords, London, UK.

Diane Coyle, diane@enlightenmenteconomics.com, Enlightenment Economics, London, UK.

Neil R. Ericsson, ericsson@frb.gov, Division of International Finance, Board of Governors of the Federal Reserve System, Washington, DC, USA.

Clive W. J. Granger, cgranger@ucsd.edu, Department of Economics, University of California at San Diego, La Jolla, California, USA.

Neal Hatch, neal.hatch@bankofengland.co.uk, Bank of England, London, UK.

David F. Hendry, david.hendry@nuffield.ox.ac.uk, Nuffield College and Department of Economics, Oxford University, Oxford, UK.

Denise R. Osborn, denise.osborn@man.ac.uk, School of Economic Studies, University of Manchester, Manchester, UK.

Marianne Sensier, marianne.sensier@man.ac.uk, School of Economic Studies, University of Manchester, Manchester, UK.

Paul W. Simpson, Paul@simp57.freeserve.co.uk, Department for Education and Employment, Sheffield, UK.

Paul Turner, p.turner@sheffield.ac.uk, Department of Economics, University of Sheffield, Sheffield, UK.

1 Editors' Introduction

Summary

This chapter introduces the topic of economic forecasting and describes the various approaches taken by this book's authors.

Historically, the theory of forecasting that underpinned actual practice in economics has been based on two key assumptions—that the model was a good representation of the economy, and that the structure of the economy would remain relatively unchanged. In reality, forecast models are mis-specified and the economy is subject to unanticipated shifts. Thus, the failure to make accurate predictions is relatively common.

In the last decade, economists have developed new theories of economic forecasting and additional methods of forecast evaluation that make less stringent assumptions. These theories and methods acknowledge that the economy is dynamic and prone to sudden shifts. They also recognize that forecasting models, however good, are greatly simplified representations that are incorrect in some respects. One advantage of these newer approaches is that we can now account for the different results of competing forecasts.

In this book's chapters, academic specialists, practitioners, and a financial journalist explain these new developments in economic forecasting. The authors discuss how forecasting is conducted, evaluated, reported, and applied by academic, private, and governmental bodies, as well as how forecasting might be taught and what costs are induced by forecast errors. The authors also describe how econometric models for forecasting are constructed, how properties of forecasting methods can be analyzed, and what the future of economic forecasting may bring.

1.1   Economic Forecasting

This chapter introduces the topic of economic forecasting. Section 1.1 (the current section) discusses forecasting in general. Section 1.2 motivates the need for forecasting and clarifies several aspects of forecasting by employing an analogy to an everyday activity—taking a trip by car. Sections 1.3 and 1.4 respectively discuss methods of forecasting and ways of evaluating or judging forecasts. Section 1.5 summarizes the remaining chapters in the book.

A forecast is a statement about the future, so forecasting is potentially a vast subject. There are two basic methods of forecasting. In the first, we have a crystal ball that can "see" into the future; in the second, we extrapolate from the present. Demonstrably functional examples of the first method appear unavailable to humanity, so we focus on the second method, restricting ourselves to *systematic* forecasting rules. Even so, there exist dozens of methods of extrapolating, as well as numerous choices of what to forecast. Many important issues thus remain to be investigated.

In the last decade, interest in economic forecasting has increased markedly. New theories of forecasting and new methods of their evaluation have been developed, and much more empirical evidence has been acquired. Drawing on these recent developments, this volume explains some of the central issues in economic forecasting.

One such issue is the uncertainty associated with forecasting. As is often remarked, the problem with forecasting is that the future is uncertain. Forecast uncertainty arises from two sources: one that we know is present and for which we understand the probabilities involved, and one due to factors that we do not even know exist. In tossing a pair of dice, the two sources might correspond to the following:

- the textbook probability that a certain pair of numbers will appear face up on any given throw, and
- the uncertainty arising from not knowing that the dice are loaded.

Clements and Hendry (1999) summarize the latter type of problem by quoting Maxine Singer.

> Because of the things [that] we don't know [that] we don't know, the future is largely unpredictable.   Singer (1997, p. 39)

Once the unpredictable has occurred, we can account for its effects, and so explain the past quite well. Indeed, most schoolchildren seem to learn history as if it were inevitable, rather than being a single and highly improbable sequence of outcomes of a complicated process in which contingency has played a large role. New unpredictable events will intrude in the future, making the future appear much more uncertain than the past.

Statistics seeks to render such individually unpredictable events as "regular" on average: that rendering underlies the theory of economic forecasting. For example, the age at which any individual person will die is uncertain, whereas the average age at death in a large population is highly predictable, and the latter observation forms the basis of the life-insurance industry. To achieve their objectives, statisticians create a model of the process in question, check how well it characterizes the evidence, and solve the model for its average outcome. Economic forecasting uses a similar principle: investigators develop models of the economy that seek to average over likely future "shocks" and so deliver a useful statement about the average future. This procedure works well for "measurable uncertainty"—that is, for the regularly occurring events that are individually unpredictable, but nevertheless average out. Singer's quote suggests that unmeasurable (or at least unmeasured) uncertainty is also important in explaining the actual uncertainty about the future.

To illustrate, imagine living in 1910 and predicting the average age at death of UK males over the period 1915–1918. Because the carnage of the First World War was not envisaged in 1910, any forecast would have been woefully inaccurate. Still, Germany could have decided against invading Belgium, in which case the United Kingdom might never have entered the war, leaving the forecast quite accurate. Or, the war might have taken an entirely different course, ending as quickly as the Franco-Prussian war of 1870–71. It is hard to imagine how anyone could conceive of the myriad possibilities that such cataclysms bring. Singer alludes to this second aspect of uncertainty, which is particularly difficult to model. In economics, events equivalent to earthquakes in geology seem to occur all too often, seriously throwing off forecasts. In the next section, an analogy closer to home helps further develop this background to economic forecasting.

1.2 An Analogy

This section motivates the need for forecasting and clarifies several aspects of forecasting, including the uncertainty inherent in forecasting, the effects of shifts in underlying economic behavior, and the costs of making forecast errors. To highlight the problems faced in economic forecasting, we draw on an commonplace activity—traveling by car.

Planning a car-trip typically involves consulting a map. Maps seek to represent connections between locations, but otherwise can seriously mislead: roads shown in red on a map are not red in reality, nor is the width of the roads to scale. Nevertheless, maps that accurately portray road connections are invaluable to planning a trip. The economic equivalent of a road map is an econometric model, which seeks to embody our best knowledge of the linkages in an economy. Evaluating a map's accuracy involves checking whether or not the roads do link up as marked on the map. Evaluating an econometric model is similar in principle, but not so easy in practice. Chapter 6 by Clive Granger considers some of the general issues involved in model evaluation, focusing primarily on the evaluation of a model's forecasts.

Given the distance to be driven, the road quality, the expected traffic density, the time of day for traveling, and the weather forecast, an initial estimate of the trip's time can be made. In many instances, that estimate will be sufficiently accurate to ensure arrival at the destination in good time. Many small factors will cause variation around this estimate: bad luck in being stopped at a sequence of traffic lights, lighter traffic than usual, and so on. The variability around the average journey time is measured by the variance of the forecast error or, more usefully, its square root, called the forecast error standard deviation. Chapter 5 by Neil Ericsson discusses such measures of forecast uncertainty. This particular measure—the forecast error standard deviation—can be expressed as a percentage of the journey time. A large value, such as 50%, denotes an unreliable route, where a journey may well take one-and-a-half times as long as expected.

Similarly, with economic forecasts, a large standard deviation for a forecast entails an unreliable forecast. To illustrate, consider the Gross Domestic Product (GDP), which is a widely used measure of the total output of a nation. Over the last 200 years, per capita GDP in many developed countries has grown at about 2% per annum, with standard deviations around that mean growth of about 3% per annum. A forecast error standard deviation larger than the average growth rate may seem poor, but substantially smaller values may be difficult to achieve in practice. Let us now see why, using our analogy to car travel.

Motorists are well aware that unexpected events can upset carefully laid plans. A crash in the traffic ahead or unexpectedly bad weather can create an extended delay, as can more extreme events, such as a bridge collapsing or an earthquake. These events do occur intermittently, and they can be viewed as rare realizations from a set of adverse factors. Their effect, however, is to shift the mean of the journey time from its norm to a much larger value; and that shift is important. An alternative route might be available, or travellers in the car could alert those already at the destination of the delay by cell phone; but otherwise the forecast error remains. Such effects are called deterministic shifts below, as they shift the mean of the variable (here, the journey time) from one value to another, and the new value persists. Economists have developed methods for handling deterministic shifts when forecasting, and Chapter 2 by David Hendry describes some of those methods. Chapter 9 by Ray Barrell examines the practical consequences of several such events, including the recent financial crisis in East Asia. In Chapter 3, Paul Turner considers how economic models can help in forecasting the effects of a specific, but important, class of shifts: changes in policy regime.

The car analogy also highlights how minor surprises can have sudden and large effects: serious traffic delays can occur, even without an extreme event as a cause. For example, when a moderate volume of traffic passes through a roadwork that reduces the number of lanes, no problems may arise. If the traffic volume increases only somewhat, horrendous congestion may result. Such effects are classified as "non-linearities" and "regime switches". Up to a point, increasing the traffic density may have only a modest effect on travel time; but beyond that point, increasing the traffic density may lead to serious delays, with gridlock as an extreme outcome. Similar situations arise in economics, causing difficulties for economic forecasters. Within a certain range, an exchange rate might respond roughly proportionally to a balance-of-payments deficit; but the exchange rate might suddenly nose-dive as concerns over bank solvency developed. As another example, booms and busts in the economy may derive from nonlinearities that generate regime switches: see Chapter 7 by Denise Osborn, Marianne Sensier, and Paul Simpson.

We now extend the travel analogy to consider additional problems in economic forecasting. Imagine that the road map is not even correct: perhaps it is out-of-date, and some roads shown on the map no longer exist. Serious forecast errors can result from following a road that unexpectedly terminates in a field. Modern economies are complex enough that no one could hope for a "correct" roadmap thereof: actual econometric models incorrectly omit important linkages and include irrelevant ones. This class of problems is called model mis-specification, and it adds to the forecasters' difficulties. In particular, model mis-specification complicates calculating the likely magnitudes of forecast errors. Sometimes, no problems ensue, as when nonexistent roads are not followed. Other times, large errors occur. For this and other reasons, some forecasting agencies maintain several models. Very different forecasts from their models warn that some of the models are at odds with reality. Actual outcomes may help isolate the source of the problem. In Chapter 8, Neal Hatch outlines the Bank of England's approach to modeling and forecasting, which includes using a suite of models rather than a single model. Later, in Chapter 10, Lord Terence Burns examines the economic consequences of making errors in forecasts from such policy models.

Returning again to the analogy of driving by car, consider a world that changed so fast that, by the time any map was available, some roads had vanished and news ones were unrecorded. Route planning would become exceptionally hazardous, and large forecast errors would abound. Estimating the forecast errors' variance would itself be hazardous, as the forecast errors would depend on which roads had vanished and which replacements could be used as substitutes. The economic forecaster confronts a similar environment, which Diane Coyle aptly and humorously characterizes in Chapter 4.

Good guides to the future are sparse when the future is not like the past. Economists refer to this situation as non-stationarity: the distribution of events changes over time. Non-stationarity is clearly a characteristic of economies: technology, legislation, politics, and society all change over time, markedly affecting living standards, the variability of unemployment and inflation, and so on. Modern econometrics devotes considerable effort to developing models of non-stationarity, and those models fall into two distinct classes. The first includes models of regular and persistent changes, or "stochastic trends"—so called because the average growth is steady but there are fluctuations around it. The second class includes models of "structural breaks", which are large sudden changes. The models with deterministic shifts, described above, are an important member of this class. Clements and Hendry (1998, 1999) provide a detailed analysis of economic forecasting when both types of change are present, along with the problems of mis-specification and data measurement error already mentioned. Structural breaks appear to explain why it is so hard to reduce forecast error standard deviations: the outcome is sometimes very far from the forecast. The 1929 crash and ensuing Great Depression is the classic example of when large forecast errors occur.

While often obvious in retrospect, many of the forecast errors that we have described resulted from unanticipated events, both large and small. Thus, in Chapter 4, Diane Coyle correctly chastises the previous UK finance minister (the Chancellor of the Exchequer) Nigel Lawson for blaming Her Majesty's Treasury for mis-forecasting over the late 1980s. Even today, the economics profession is not unanimous on which factors induced those forecast errors, although many believe that financial deregulation was responsible, as it led to an unexpectedly sharp reduction in credit rationing. Unanticipated events, like the sudden rise of oil prices in 2000, do occur; and they thereby disrupt forecast accuracy. However, not all methods of forecasting are equally disrupted. Thus, we now turn to how forecasting is done (Section 1.3) and how forecasts are evaluated (Section 1.4).

1.3 Forecasting Methods

Forecasts are *constructed*, and many methods are available for constructing them. In our extensive analogy, the forecast of the trip's time was based on the distance (measured on the map) and average speed (dependent on road quality and traffic conditions), mediated by any likely special factors. If the map is inaccurate, so may be the forecasts. That said, a poor model need not lead to inaccurate forecasts. For example, the Ptolemaic system is hardly a realistic model of planetary motions, but nonetheless it predicts lunar eclipses reasonably well. A map likewise may have always been incorrect, with corresponding forecasts for trip times wrong, but no worse than usual. Equally, a map may have become incorrect because a bridge was closed. That sort of event leads to "forecast failure", where a previously well-performing approach suddenly does much worse.

For repeated journeys, an alternative forecasting method is available, and it does not rely on a map at all: forecast the journey's time by how long it took on the previous occasion. If the road network does not change, and if no special factors disturbed the previous journey, then such a pure extrapolation could be quite accurate, and it is independent of how good or bad the map is. If the relation between the map and reality is poor, or if that relation continually alters, then extrapolating the previous outcome may be as accurate as one can achieve.

These situations parallel those faced by economists when forecasting: models are far from accurate representations of the economy, and their accuracy frequently changes abruptly. A model that closely represents the economy is a good basis for forecasting only if the future economy is "close" to the current one. The culprit of forecast failure is not rapid evolution *per se*, as commonly occurs in technology, but abrupt changes, as may derive from legislative and political developments. In such a setting, a model structured around past economic behavior may not be the best forecasting device available. Rather, a "naive predictor" that simply extrapolates from previous outcomes may be more successful. If the economy stays on track, such extrapolative forecasts are generally accurate. If the economy crashes, the extrapolative forecast will miss the crash itself, as typically will other types of forecasts. However, once the crash has occurred, the extrapolative forecast tends to come back on track, whereas many other types of forecast models continue to mis-forecast systematically. Consequently, it is desirable that forecasts from economic models "adapt", with those forecasts adjusting rapidly to major changes, even when those changes are unpredictable. A particularly damning criticism of historical forecast errors is how *systematic* those forecast errors have been—not that the forecast errors were sometimes large. For the United Kingdom, long sequences of under-prediction and over-prediction have been recorded: the Chancellor of the Exchequer may have been right to complain about those.

Reverting to our analogy, modern technology has developed instruments for informing drivers about congestion on the road ahead, so drivers can adapt more easily, as by selecting a diversion before becoming stuck in a traffic jam, whatever its source. Such flexibility enhances their probability of correctly forecasting the overall journey time. Of course, really major shocks might disrupt even that provision of information.

Different approaches are available for modeling rare events and accounting for them in forecasting. Preferably, we would forecast the rare events directly in order to avoid large forecast errors for other variables that depend upon those rare events. As Osborn, Sensier, and Simpson document in Chapter 7, modeling and forecasting rare events can be particularly onerous, simply because there are so few observations on the rare events themselves. Another approach, just discussed, is to rapidly adjust forecasts to the shocks, or to build models that are resilient to large shocks. A third approach is to model the rare events, see how often they occurred and how big they were, and modify the forecasts accordingly. Two forecasts might be produced, one accounting for and the other neglecting some large potential shock, such as another oil crisis. Each person can then select the forecast that he or she deems most likely. Or, the two forecasts can be averaged, weighted by how likely the shock (or its absence) is believed to be. To illustrate that by our analogy, one might expect a 4-hour journey without delays and a 6-hour journey (equally likely) with delays, and so schedule 5 hours total in order to allow for both possible outcomes. Note that actual outcomes always differ from the weighted forecast in this case—the actual journey time is either 4 hours or 6 hours and never the 5 hours planned. Whether or not discrepancies between forecasts and outcomes matter depends on the costs of forecast errors.

1.4 Evaluating Forecasts

Typically, forecasts are made to aid a decision, so it is natural to judge forecasts in that context. In terms of our analogy, the goal may be to arrive home before dinner: allowing for contingencies can help ensure a timely arrival. Depending upon the decision and the costs faced, inaccuracy in the forecasts may or may not matter. Chapter 6—by Clive Granger—considers these issues in some detail, while Chapter 5 by Neil Ericsson focuses on measuring and understanding the uncertainty associated with forecast errors, and Chapter 10 by Lord Terence Burns examines the costs of forecast errors for economic policy.

Many macroeconomic forecasts are made with little knowledge about the likely decision makers, who may be in government, business, or even resident in a different country. One conventional measure for comparing forecast outcomes is the mean square forecast error, which weights the forecasts' accuracy ("how close") and its precision ("how volatile"). In Chapter 2, David Hendry examines some difficulties with this measure. In Chapter 4, Diane Coyle discusses the criteria she used for granting *The Independent* newspaper's Golden Guru award for the year's best economic forecasts.

1.5 Summary of the Chapters

This section summarizes the remaining chapters in the book, chapter by chapter, interrelating their themes to the ones just discussed. For convenience, figures (which are central to many of the chapters' discussions) often appear as panels of graphs, with each graph in a panel labeled sequentially by a suffix $a, b, c, \ldots$, left to right, row by row.

Chapter 2—*How Economists Forecast*, by **David Hendry**—raises ten questions central to forecasting:

What is a forecast?
What can be forecast?
How is forecasting done generally?
How is forecasting done by economists?
How can one measure the success or failure of forecasts?
How confident can we be in such forecasts?
How do we analyze the properties of forecasting methods?
What are the main problems in economic forecasting?
Do these problems have potential solutions?
What is the future of economic forecasting?

To answer these questions, Hendry examines the notion of a forecast in general and reviews various forecasting methods used by economists.

He then discusses some difficulties that arise when evaluating forecast accuracy, leading to an empirical illustration in which he models and forecasts UK industrial output over the last three centuries. For Hendry, the main problem in economic forecasting is systematic forecast failure that is induced by data non-stationarity. Potential solutions exist, and Hendry sees a promising future for economic forecasting with econometric systems.

Chapter 3—*Economic Modeling for Fun and Profit*, by **Paul Turner**—considers the role of economics in models that generate economic forecasts. He discusses the advantages that a model based on economic theory has relative to a pure time-series model, illustrating those advantages with forecasts of the UK's Gross Domestic Product. In economic forecasting, the primary benefit of a more fully specified model arises in the analysis of economic policy, where the government adjusts policy variables such as the interest rate and tax rates, which themselves affect the course of the economy. Policy shifts thus can alter economic forecasts. Turner develops a simple but fully articulated model of the UK economy to illustrate how forecasts can be generated under different policy regimes.

Chapter 4—*Making Sense of Published Economic Forecasts*, by **Diane Coyle**—focuses directly on the theme of our book. For some time, Coyle has given the Golden Guru award to the year's best forecaster of the UK's "misery index", which is an index that depends upon inflation, unemployment, and economic growth. She finds that forecasters herd together on these three key measures, with the Golden Guru award being won by only a narrow margin and with very few repeat winners. She humorously describes the forecasters' task and considers how journalists could improve their presentations of forecasts, as by avoiding spurious precision and by explaining carefully the uncertainties involved in forecasts. Coyle also examines additional difficulties associated with forecasts in the conduct of economic policy.

Chapter 5—*Forecast Uncertainty in Economic Modeling*, by **Neil Ericsson**—defines forecast uncertainty, examines various measures of forecast uncertainty, and analyzes some of the sources and consequences of forecast uncertainty. Forecast uncertainty reflects the dispersion of possible outcomes around the forecast made, and that uncertainty can be measured in many ways. Ericsson emphasizes the distinction noted above between "what we don't know that we don't know" and "what we do know that we don't know", since only uncertainty arising from the latter can be calculated when constructing measures of forecast uncertainty. In practice, forecast uncertainty also depends upon what is being forecast, the model used for forecasting, the actual economic process, and the forecast horizon. Ericsson highlights these empirical sources of forecast uncertainty and their consequences with examples involving the US trade balance, UK inflation, UK real national income, and the US/UK exchange rate.

Chapter 6—*Evaluation of Forecasts*, by **Clive Granger**—discusses economic model evaluation in general, stressing that the evaluation criteria should depend on the purpose of the model. Granger then applies this principle to forecast evaluation. Forecasts are made for a purpose, with those forecasts typically entailing economic decisions and with the resulting forecast errors entailing economic costs. Different models generate different forecasts, and the resulting economic costs have different distributions, which can be compared across models.

Chapter 7—*Forecasting and the UK Business Cycle*, by **Denise Osborn**, **Marianne Sensier**, and **Paul Simpson**—shows that forecasting economic activity over the business cycle is an exacting task. Because recessions are relatively rare events, only a few observations on them are available, and that makes modeling recessions particularly difficult. The authors propose a class of regime-switching models, with a short-term interest rate as a leading indicator to provide predictive information about future regimes. They find that large increases in the interest rate raise the probability of switching out of an expansion into a recession a year later, whereas, in a recession, even small decreases in interest rates help start a recovery. Their analysis highlights the importance of the interest-rate decisions taken by the Monetary Policy Committee (MPC) at the Bank of England, and the need for the MPC to look well ahead when making interest-rate decisions.

On exactly that theme, Chapter 8—*Modeling and Forecasting at the Bank of England*, by **Neal Hatch**—describes how modeling and forecasting at the Bank provide a key input to the MPC's deliberations. Because monetary policy affects output and inflation with a lag, a forward-looking approach is essential for successful inflation targeting in particular and for monetary policymaking generally. Economic models help the MPC make its forecasts for output growth and inflation, and the MPC's own projections are published in the Bank's quarterly *Inflation Report*. Models also aid thinking about monetary policy in general, as when simulating how the economy might be affected by possible changes in the way that inflation expectations are formed. Hatch describes how forecasts are made by Bank staff and how those forecasts feed into the MPC's judgments. The Bank's models are tools to help thinking about economic problems, and different models are needed for different purposes, reiterating Clive Granger's message in Chapter 6 from a different perspective.

Chapter 9—*Forecasting the World Economy*, by **Ray Barrell**—draws on Barrell's many years of forecast experience at the UK's National Institute of Economic and Social Research. Barrell focuses on the problems of endemic structural change, the importance of using a structural econometric model to interpret shifts, and the consequent role of judgment when forming forecasts. He highlights these themes with empirical illustrations of unexpected structural changes involving both deteriorations to and improvements in economic conditions. Recent deteriorations include the East Asian crisis in 1997 and 1998, the changing structure of capital flows, and the collapse of the Long Term Capital Management (LTCM) hedge fund in September 1998. Improvements include the effects from living in a low-inflation world, with the associated reduction of inflation uncertainty in the United Kingdom.

Chapter 10—*The Costs of Forecast Errors*, by **Lord Terence Burns**—provides a fascinating and insightful discussion on the costs associated with making errors in forecasts. Lord Burns draws on 15 years' experience forecasting at the London Business School and nearly two decades' experience in the UK government, first as Chief Economic Adviser at Her Majesty's Treasury and then as Permanent Secretary. After arguing for articulated econometric models along lines similar to those in Chapters 3 and 9, Lord Burns analyzes the empirical characteristics of forecast errors. Forecast errors are largest when the most is happening in the economy. Forecast errors are correlated across variables; and they reflect external shocks—which were often not forecast—and inaccurate data about the recent past. These sources are among those suggested by the theory in Chapter 11. Overall, Lord Burns feels that the economics profession has made very little progress in reducing the size of forecast errors over the past 30 years or so, although he recognizes that such a lack of improvement may mirror the growing complexities of modern economies.

Lord Burns then considers the implications of forecast errors, both within a given policy framework and for the choice of the policy framework. Within a given policy framework, forecast errors may increase instability and hence have a longer-term effect on economic performance. In that light, he discusses the present inflation-targeting arrangements in terms of where forecast errors might arise and what their costs might be, especially for the credibility of the policy regime. Changes in policy regime tend to arise only infrequently—the United Kingdom has experienced only six major changes in policy regime since the mid-1970s. Lord Burns concludes that forecast errors are important to consider in the conduct of policy, and that better forecasts will allow economic gains. Thus, the search for improved forecasting models and methods should continue.

Chapter 11—the *Epilogue*—reviews what we have learned from this excursion into economic forecasting and how this journey has helped clarify our understanding of economic forecasts. In doing so, the epilogue provides a unified perspective of the book's chapters, drawing on additional recent results from the literature on economic forecasting.

2   How Economists Forecast

David F. Hendry

Summary

This chapter considers ten questions about economic forecasting, namely: What is a forecast? What can be forecast? How is forecasting done generally? How is forecasting done by economists? How can one measure the success or failure of forecasts? How confident can we be in such forecasts? How do we analyze the properties of forecasting methods? What are the main problems in economic forecasting? Do these problems have potential solutions? What is the future of economic forecasting? To resolve these questions, this chapter first considers the general notion of a forecast, and then reviews the various forecasting methods used by economists. Difficulties in evaluating forecast accuracy are discussed, followed by an empirical illustration of forecast properties. The main problem in economic forecasting is systematic forecast failure induced by the non-stationarity of economic data, as an analysis of UK industrial output since 1700 demonstrates. That analysis also suggests a promising future for economic forecasting with econometric systems because—despite their present travails—there are solutions to their most serious problems.

2.1 Introduction

A forecast is a statement about the future. Such statements may be derived from statistical models or informal methods. Forecasts may be well based or badly based, accurate or inaccurate, precise or imprecise; and they may concern short-term or long horizons. Thus, forecasting is potentially a vast topic. To focus the analysis, we address the following ten questions about forecasting:

- What is a forecast?
- What can be forecast?
- How is forecasting done generally?
- How is forecasting done by economists?
- How can one measure the success or failure of forecasts?
- How confident can we be in such forecasts?
- How do we analyze the properties of forecasting methods?
- What are the main problems in economic forecasting?
- Do these problems have potential solutions?
- What is the future of economic forecasting?

Section 2.2 introduces forecasting through the wide range of expressions in the English language for forecasts and forecasters. This section also draws an important distinction between forecasting and predicting: anything can be forecast, but not everything can be predicted. Section 2.3 provides some essential background for Section 2.4, which describes the main methods of forecasting that have been used in economics. Forecasts may be produced by methods ranging from well-tested empirical econometric systems to methods with no observable basis (such as forecasting the 2005 Derby horse-race winner in June 1999); Section 2.5 discusses the potential merits of some of these approaches. Howsoever forecasts are produced, one might expect that their accuracy could always be gauged. Unfortunately, there is no unique measure for the accuracy of an economic forecast, as Section 2.6 demonstrates; and there is no guarantee that better based methods will win in forecasting competitions. Section 2.7 notes some factors that might influence our confidence in economic forecasts.

Section 2.8 then considers how economists analyze their methods. To do so, this section contrasts forecasts from an empirical model with those based on artificial computer-generated data. Section 2.9 discusses why the main problems in economic forecasting arise from relatively sudden, intermittent, large shifts in the behavior of the time series. We call such shifts structural breaks. To illustrate, Section 2.10 analyzes UK industrial output since 1700. Historically, growth rates of output have altered dramatically. We consider the plight of a mythical, long-lived economist who has been given the task of forecasting UK industrial output over each half-century starting in 1750, and we examine how often she would have been badly wrong. By comparing the outcomes from different methods, Section 2.11 suggests some potential solutions to such forecast failures. Section 2.12 concludes, briefly considering the future of economic forecasting.

2.2 Forecast Terminology

This section surveys the wide range of expressions in the English language for forecasts and forecasters. This section also draws an important distinction between forecasting and predicting—a distinction used throughout this book.

English is a rich language, and it reaches one of its peaks of verbosity with synonyms for "forecasting". This may be because *ante-*, *pre-*, and *fore-* offer an abundance of prefixes. We can construct such interesting sentences as the following.

> The foresightful oracle of Delphi spoke "Those who can, do; those who can't, forecast" when she divined the future to foretell the prophecy by a soothsayer whose premonitions included the expectation that one day economists would be able to predict the effects of economic policy.

"Forecast" has an interesting etymology: the meaning of *fore-* is clear, denoting "in front" or "in advance". The interesting bit is *-cast*: dice, lots, spells (as in to bewitch), and horoscopes are all said to be "cast". Together with "casting a fly", these meanings suggest "chancing one's luck", as does "cast about", and perhaps the older usage of "casting accounts". Such connections link the notion of forecasting to gamblers and perhaps even to charlatans. In fact, this is true of many of the other synonyms for forecast, forecasters, and forecasting, which include: augury, Cassandra (prophesy without credibility), clairvoyance (seeing things not present to the senses), foreboding, foresee, foreshadow, omen (sign of a future event), precognition (knowing before the occurrence), presage (to indicate an event yet to happen), prescience (foreknowledge), portend (to warn in advance), scry (to practice crystal-gazing), and seer (one who sees into the future). At this point, I quit on this almost endless list.

Most of these synonyms have an air of doom about them, so we may conclude that forecasting has been a disreputable occupation since time immemorial. Some synonyms have yet to acquire adverse connotations, as with anticipate (to look forward to, and originally derived from *ante*—not related to *anti-*, which means "against"—and *capere*, meaning "to take"), extrapolate (to extend the current trend), prognosis (prediction of the course of a disease), and project (to predict on the basis of past results or present trends). Still, it would hardly improve the credibility of weather forecasting or economic forecasting to rename them as weather soothsaying or economic scrying.

Dictionaries do sometimes treat the words forecast and predict as synonyms: "forecast: reckon beforehand, or conjecture about the future", as against "predict: forecast, foretell, or prophesy". Even so, common usage suggests that the two words have somewhat different senses, as with weather forecasting, not weather prediction. Equally, one might observe that it was predictable that a marriage would fail, but not forecastable when it would do so. Webster suggests that predict implies inference from laws of nature, whereas forecast is more probabilistic. This most nearly matches the way that I want to use the terms. Whether or not an event is predictable is a property of that event, irrespective of our ability to actually predict it. By contrast, an event is always forecastable, since a forecast is simply a statement about the event. It thus makes sense to talk about forecasting an unpredictable event—indeed, many say that has always been true of British weather!

There has long been a market for foreknowledge, with insider trading being but a recent example. Economics teaches us that "the bigger the market the greater the supply", and the current book corroborates that prediction. Also, older words for the concept of "making a statement about a future event" and for anyone who makes such statements do tend to have less scientific connotations: prophesy, oracle, seer, soothsayer, and charlatan. Because "forecasting" does not currently have a great reputation, perhaps we should coin a new word, such as ante-stating, fore-dicting, or pre-telling. Precasting has been preempted by cement makers and previewing by the media, and prevision already has a well-established usage.

Literature has occasionally addressed the topics of forecasting and prediction, as Shakespeare did in *Macbeth* (I, iii):

> If you can look into the seeds of time
> And say which grain will grow and which will not,
> Speak then to me.

For the seeds of plants, meeting that request may even be possible with modern technology, in so far as the seed's DNA, inbuilt sustenance, and so on could be determined by some appropriate scanning device. Shelley was less inscrutable in *Ode to the West Wind* (1, 57):

> Scatter as from an unextinguished hearth
> Ashes and sparks, my words among mankind!
> Be through my lips to unawakened earth
> The trumpet of a prophecy! O Wind,
> If Winter comes, can Spring be far behind?

Here we have a very reliable forecast, or at least one not yet refuted on thousands of repetitions. Thus, both literary examples may actually prove successful, unlike much of economic forecasting.

The trouble with forecasting is that the future is uncertain; and it is uncertain for two reasons.[1] Maxine Singer (1997, p. 39) succinctly captures both reasons for forecast uncertainty in her "Thoughts of a Nonmillenarian". She describes the first reason as follows:

> Because of the things we don't know [that] we don't know,
> the future is largely unpredictable.

Notice her wording. It is not that the future is unforecastable: clearly, the future is forecastable, and many statements prognosticating on future possibilities appear daily. Rather, it is that the future is largely unpredictable. Singer then continues, describing the second reason for forecast uncertainty:

> But some developments can be anticipated, or at least imagined, on the basis of existing knowledge.

This second reason is responsible for the apparent randomness of outcomes within the realms that we do understand—we call this measurable uncertainty. The first source of uncertainty is the basic problem. The second source may even make us overly confident about our forecasts, as we will see in later sections.

---

[1] The uncertainty of the future is also the main attraction of forecasting: we can make a living from forecasting, while staying sane by not knowing what the future holds in store.

2.3 Some Essential Background

This section notes various ways in which actual economies alter over time, and it considers some of the implications that those changes have for economic forecasting. Economies evolve over time and are also subject to intermittent, and sometimes large, unanticipated shocks. Economic evolution has its source in scientific discoveries and inventions, which lead to technical progress, which itself becomes embodied in physical and human capital. By contrast, changes in legislation, sudden switches in economic policy, and political turmoil may precipitate large shocks or "breaks" in the economy. Examples of breaks relevant to the United Kingdom include the abolition of exchange controls, the introduction of interest-bearing checking accounts, and the privatization of government-owned enterprises. Because of both evolution and intermittent large shocks, economic data are not stationary, in that measured economic data have means and variances that alter over time.

Non-stationary data are exceptionally difficult to model because their means and variances are changing over time. Consequently, the empirical econometric models used to understand and forecast processes as complicated as entire national economies are far from perfect representations of economic behavior. Forecasters may be only dimly aware of what change is afoot. Even when new developments can be envisaged, forecasters may find it hard to quantify the likely effects.[2] Moreover, the data series used in economic model-building are often inaccurate and subject to revision.

All these difficulties entail that economic forecasting is fraught with problems and that forecast failure—a significant deterioration in forecast performance relative to the anticipated outcome—is all too common in practice. Understanding this phenomenon requires a theory of economic forecasting in which forecast models are incorrect in unknown ways and the economy itself is complicated, changing over time, and measured by inaccurate data. A theory based on these realistic assumptions has been developed recently, and that theory's main

---

[2] For example, recently in the United Kingdom, a group of non-profit organizations called Building Societies (similar to Savings and Loans Associations in the United States) demutualized by becoming limited-liability commercial Banks, and distributed the proceeds as windfall gains to their customers: the impact on consumers' spending of that largess was unclear for several years.

implications have demonstrable empirical relevance; see Clements and Hendry (1998, 1999). Unfortunately, many of the conclusions established for *correctly* specified forecasting models of *stationary* processes do not hold in this more general setting. Fortunately, the new theory suggests ways of circumventing systematic forecast failure in economics.

Poor forecasting is distinct from forecast failure. Some variables may be inherently uncertain: while forecasts of these variables are poor absolutely, we are not suddenly confronted by large (or at least much larger) forecast errors. Because economic forecasts may alter actions of individuals in the economy, some events may be inherently unpredictable, such as changes in equity prices and (perhaps) exchange-rate crises. We thus should not expect anything other than poor forecasts of unpredictable events, but we may hope to avoid systematic forecast failure; see Section 2.9.

Econometric forecasting models are systems of relationships between variables such as GNP, inflation, money, interest rates, and exchange rates. The relationships or "equations" in these models are then estimated from available data, which are mainly aggregate time series. These models have three main components:

- *deterministic terms* (such as intercepts—taking the values 1, 1, 1, ... — and linear trends—taking the values 1, 2, 3, ...), which are introduced to capture averages and steady growth, and whose future values are known;
- *observed stochastic variables* (such as consumers' expenditure, prices, and output), which have unknown future values; and
- *unobserved errors*, all of whose values—past, present, and future— are unknown, although perhaps estimable in the context of a model.

Relationships involving any of these three components could be inappropriately formulated or inaccurately estimated, or could alter over time in unanticipated ways. Each of the resulting nine types of mistake *could* induce poor forecast performance through either inaccurate (i.e., biased) or imprecise (i.e., high-variance) forecasts. That said, theory suggests that some types of mistakes have pernicious effects on forecasts, whereas others are relatively benign in most settings. Surprisingly, the key to understanding systematic forecast failure depends on the behavior of the deterministic terms—even though their future values are known—rather than on the behavior of variables with unknown future values.

Five aspects of the deterministic terms matter in practice. First, their specification and estimation matter: inadequate representations or inaccurate estimates of intercepts and trends can induce bad forecasts. Knowing the future values of the trend is of little help when it is multiplied by the wrong parameter value. For example, omitting a trend in a model when there is a trend in the data leads to ever-increasing forecast errors. Second, unanticipated changes in the values of deterministic terms have pernicious consequences: the economy moves, but the model's forecasts do not, thereby inducing large forecast errors. Thus, although the future values of the existing deterministic variables are known, there may be different coefficients on intercepts and trends in the future, and those values are not currently known: see the quote above from Singer (1997). Third, deterministic shifts may reflect changes elsewhere in the economy that are interacting with an incomplete model specification. Fourth, formulating models to minimize the effects of possible changes in deterministic terms is generally beneficial for forecasting, even when the cost is a poorer representation by the model of both the economic theory and the data. Finally, successful modeling of changes in deterministic terms pays handsome dividends, even if only by using simple corrections or updates.

Figure 2.1 portrays four forecasting problems involving deterministic variables. In the top left panel, the wrong slope of the trend has been estimated. In the top right panel, the intercept has shifted, so the sample mean is wrong in both regimes. In the lower left panel, the data trend has changed but the model has not. The lower right panel plots the temporal changes of the trend and forecasts in the previous panel, illustrating that the first differences of those series differ mainly at the jump point.

Other possible sources of forecast errors—such as mis-specifying the stochastic components, or uncertainty due to estimating their parameters—appear less important. Thus, this new forecast theory directs attention to areas that may induce forecast failure, and it casts serious doubt on competing explanations of predictive failure, such as inadequate use of economic theory. For instance, the new forecast theory

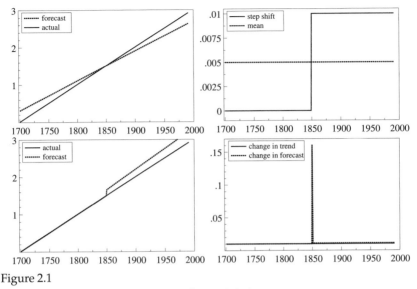

Figure 2.1

The effects of incorrect or changing deterministic terms.

offers no support for claims that imposing restrictions from economic theory will improve forecast accuracy; cf. Diebold (1998).

As an indirect consequence, there may be little gain in forecast accuracy by inventing "better" estimation methods, especially if the opportunity cost of doing so is less effort devoted to developing forecasting models that are more robust to shifts in deterministic terms. The new forecast theory also suggests that selecting a model from the data should have a minimal effect on forecast failure, as should estimating unnecessary parameters, unless sample sizes are very small.[3]

Forecast confidence intervals seek to measure forecast uncertainty, but they reflect only the "known uncertainties", which derive from model estimation and from future shocks that resemble those in the past. While these known sources of forecast uncertainty may be important, unanticipated deterministic shifts occur intermittently in economics and will also contribute to forecast uncertainty. Because we

---

[3]Retaining irrelevant variables that then change can induce forecast failure, but, in a progressive research strategy, such variables will be eliminated when the model is re-estimated over the enlarged sample.

don't know what we don't know, it is difficult to account for "unknown uncertainty". Nevertheless, the new forecast theory indicates ways of avoiding *systematic* forecast failure when economies are subject to sudden, unanticipated, large shifts. The UK economy has witnessed many such shifts in the last century, and there is no sign that large shocks are abating. When shocks are unanticipated, it would take a magician to avoid large errors from forecasts made *before* such shocks have occurred. Rather, given an inability to forecast the shock, adaptation in the forecast process is required, once a shock has occurred, in order to avoid a *sequence* of poor forecasts.

2.4 Methods of Forecasting

This section thus turns to the main methods of forecasting that have been used in economics. An econometric model provides one way of making economic forecasts; many other ways are also available. The success of economic forecasts, whatever their source, requires that:

(a) there are regularities to be captured,
(b) the regularities are informative about the future,
(c) the proposed method captures those regularities, and yet
(d) it excludes non-regularities.

Items (a) and (b) are characteristics of the economic system, whereas items (c) and (d) are characteristics of the forecasting method. The history of economic forecasting in the United Kingdom suggests that there are some regularities which are informative about future events, but also that there are major irregularities; see Burns (1986), Wallis (1989), Pain and Britton (1992), Cook (1995), and Clements and Hendry (2001b) *inter alia*. However, achieving (c) jointly with (d) is difficult in practice.

Methods of forecasting include:

- guessing, "rules of thumb", and "informal models";
- extrapolation;
- leading indicators;
- surveys;
- time-series models; and
- econometric systems.

Each of these approaches is common in practice, so it is helpful to review their advantages and disadvantages.

Guessing and related methods rely on luck alone. While that may be a minimal assumption compared to other methods, guessing is not generally a useful method, even if, at every point in time, *some* oracle manages to forecast accurately. Unfortunately, no one can predict which oracle will be successful next.

Extrapolation is fine for forecasting, so long as the extrapolated tendencies actually persist, but that itself is doubtful. The telling feature is that different extrapolators are used at different points in time. Moreover, forecasts are most useful when they predict changes in tendencies, and extrapolative methods can never do so. To wit, many a person has bought a house at the peak of a housing boom, only to see the housing market slump thereafter.

Forecasting based on *leading indicators* is unreliable unless the reasons for the lead are clear, as with orders leading production. As an example of their unreliability, the Harvard Barometer (a well-known leading indicator) missed the 1929 collapse. In practice, leading indicators need to be changed regularly, highlighting their inability to capture many of the underlying changes in the economy.

Surveys of consumers and businesses can be informative about future events. However, surveys rely on the interviewees' plans being realized. If plans aren't realized, surveys usually can offer only *ad hoc* explanations for the discrepancies between plans and outcomes.

Historically, *time-series models* have forecast quite well, relative to econometric systems. The theory discussed in Section 2.3 offers an explanation for that result in terms of their relative robustness to deterministic shifts, as illustrated in Figure 2.1. We also will use several simple time-series models below as examples.

Econometric forecasting models were described in Section 2.3 above. Formal econometric systems of national economies consolidate existing empirical and theoretical knowledge of how economies function; they provide a framework for a progressive research strategy; they provide forecasts and policy advice; and (in conjunction with the new forecasting theory) they help explain their own failures. Econometric and time-series models are the primary methods of forecasting in economics.

2.5   On Winning at Forecasting

What determines the winners and losers in a forecasting competition? Many factors undoubtedly play a role, but one aspect can be illustrated by the following example, in which two friends—Sue and Peter—are passing time while waiting at a bus stop. Sue challenges Peter to forecast the behavior of a student who is also standing inside the bus shelter: every minute, Sue and Peter will both write down a forecast as to whether or not the student will be in the bus shelter in a minute's time. Peter is an economist, so he uses a causal model: students stand at bus stops to get on buses. Thus, if no bus approaches, Peter forecasts that the student will stay; but when a bus appears, Peter forecasts that the student will board the bus and hence will be gone. Sue, however, has been to my lectures on forecasting, so she always writes what the current situation is: when the student is there, she forecasts he will still be there in a minute's time; when he has left, she forecasts that he will still not be there in a minute's time.

During the first 10 minutes, four different buses come by, and the student remains stubbornly at the bus stop. Then his girl friend appears on her motor bike, the student climbs on, and they go away. Peter is wrong 4 times in the first 10 minutes. Furthermore, if he sticks to his causal model, he is wrong ever after, as the student never got on a bus. Sue, however, is correct 10 times in the first 10 minutes, then wrong once when the student leaves, and then correct again forever thereafter.

Thus, to win a forecasting competition in the face of unanticipated outcomes, simply forecast the present, where the present is perhaps transformed to a stationary distribution. Causal models can go badly wrong in any given instance, and they need rapid repair when they do go wrong. However, the vacuous nature of Sue's forecast is clear, even though she did win: replace the phrase "the student will remain at the bus stop" by the phrase "the volcano Mount St. Helens will not erupt". Thus, economists are right to stick to causal modeling as a basis for forecasting, perhaps mediating their forecasts by adjustments to offset the unanticipated, should it eventuate.

We should be pleased with forecast failures, as we learn greatly from them. We should not be ashamed to admit that we lack a full understanding of how economies behave. Thus, I reiterate an old complaint: when weather forecasts go awry, meteorologists get a new super-computer; when economists mis-forecast, we get our budgets cut.

2.6   On Determining the Forecast Winner

Surprisingly, there generally is no unique measure for the accuracy of an economic forecast, as this section now discusses.

A forecast's accuracy and its precision represent different dimensions of forecasting. Precision almost always denotes "with little uncertainty": one can say that the moon is exactly 5,000 miles from the Earth and be very precise, and also very inaccurate. Conversely, it is accurate to say that the moon lies between 1,000 and 1,000,000 miles away, but this statement is also very imprecise.

To measure accuracy and precision, we usually adopt two concepts: unbiasedness, under which the forecasts are centered on the outcomes; and a small variance, implying that only a narrow range of outcomes is compatible with the forecast. A natural combination of bias and variance leads to the measure of mean square forecast error (MSFE), which is commonly reported in many forecast comparisons.

Unfortunately, even with an agreed-upon metric such as the MSFE, no clearcut "winner" necessarily results in a forecasting competition that involves either multi-period or multi-variable forecasts. Both multi-period and multi-variable forecasts are the norm in economics. Figure 2.2 illustrates the problem. A given forecast (denoted forecast *a*) is awful for the levels of the series shown (top left panel), but is reasonably accurate for the growth rate of the series (top right panel). Conversely, forecast *b* is fine for the level of the series (lower left panel), but dreadful for the growth rate (lower right panel). Thus, before it is even possible to choose the winner, one must select the aspect about which it is important to be close. Worse still, the MSFE itself is not an obvious criterion: a stockbroker probably does not care how good or bad a model is on MSFE if the model is the best available for making money!

2.7   Forecast Confidence Intervals

Forecasts are sometimes presented with estimates of the uncertainty attached to them. One common form is a forecast confidence interval that

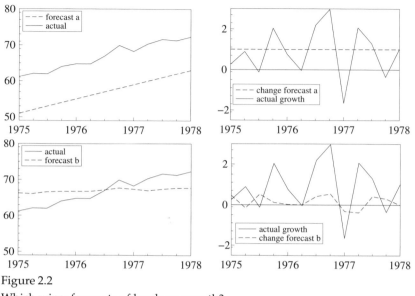

Figure 2.2

Which wins: forecasts of levels or growth?.

is expected to cover the likely outcomes some percentage of the time, such as 67% or 95%. Naturally, forecast confidence intervals tend to be wider for longer forecast horizons. The Bank of England's fan charts for their inflation forecasts (sometimes called "rivers of blood") show ranges of intervals in ever lighter shades of red as the likelihood of the outcome lying outside each bound falls; see Chapter 8. Such estimates of forecast uncertainty are very much welcome, especially when the alternative is merely presenting a forecast number (e.g., "2% inflation"), reported as if it were exact. Surprisingly, reporting of forecasts alone was the norm for the Bank, even until relatively recently; and it still is the norm among many forecasters. In Section 2.8 below, Figures 2.3 and 2.4 highlight the importance of reporting measures of forecast uncertainty, with Figure 2.4 including fan charts that show decreasing probabilities by lighter shades.

Because the future is uncertain, outcomes can at best lie within some interval around a forecast. Even when a forecast confidence interval is correctly calculated, outcomes should lie outside that range the converse percentage of the time. For instance, for a 67% interval, outcomes should lie outside that interval 33% of the time. As stressed above, however, reported intervals are based on "known uncertainties" and cannot reflect "what we don't know we don't know". Nor is this problem unique to economics: Gould (2000, Ch.10) discusses the difficulty of forecasting in the face of "the unpredictability of evolutionary and social futures". Thus, forecasters sometimes will do worse than they anticipate from their conventional calculations; see Chapter 5. While "unknown uncertainties" need not entail a lack of confidence in forecasts, they emphasize the considerable uncertainty attached to possible future outcomes and the corresponding tentative nature of forecasts.

2.8 How Economists Analyze Their Methods

To illustrate how economists analyze their methods, this section examines both forecasts from an empirical econometric model and forecasts based on artificial computer-generated data. Econometric methods are derived under various assumptions about how economies function, and these assumptions may not be appropriate. Simulation methods have proved useful for checking the adequacy of econometric models and methods. In such simulations, we construct a facsimile of the econometric model on the computer and compare the properties of the data that it produces with actual outcomes. A serious mismatch reveals hidden inadequacies. Lets us undertake an example.

To start, one must produce an empirical model of the time series to be forecast. Here, we consider a small monetary system comprising UK narrow money (the M1 measure, denoted m), total final expenditure in 1985 prices (a demand measure, denoted x), its implicit deflator (the price level, denoted p), and the opportunity cost of holding narrow money (the difference between the short-term market interest rate and the interest rate paid on checking accounts, and denoted R).[4] Below, lowercase letters denote logarithms (in base e) of the original variables, and Δ denotes the change in a variable. These four variables are transformed to the variables $m - p$, x, Δp, and R, with the first $(m - p)$

---

[4]This dataset is much studied, and with many contributors; see *inter alia* Hendry (1979), Ericsson, Campos and Tran (1990), Hendry and Ericsson (1991), Johansen (1992), Hendry and Mizon (1993), Hendry and Doornik (1994), Paroulo (1996), Doornik, Hendry and Nielsen (1998), and Rahbek, Kongsted and Jørgensen (1999).

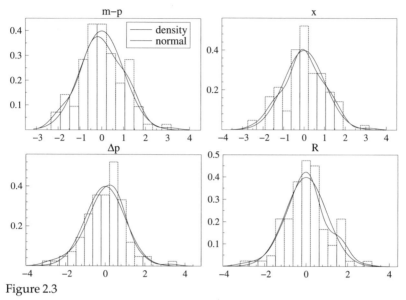
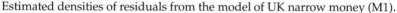

Figure 2.3
Estimated densities of residuals from the model of UK narrow money (M1).

being the log of real money and the third (Δp) being inflation. The transformed variables are modeled as a function of their previous values (to account for dynamic adjustment), indicator variables (to capture large policy changes such as oil shocks and budget shifts), and past excess demands for money and for goods and services (modeled by deviations from long-run relations, and found by cointegration analysis). The estimated parameters characterize the speeds of adjustment in removing disequilibria in excess demands, as well as the responses to past changes and major shocks. The properties of the unexplained components (the residuals) represent the assumed innovation shocks.

Figure 2.3 quantitatively measures the degree to which the model is unable to explain the data in sample. Specifically, Figure 2.3 shows the histograms and approximating densities of the four sets of residuals (standardized to a unit variance) from the equations estimated over 1964–1989. Figure 2.3 also plots the density for the normal distribution, which provides a reasonable approximation to the residuals' densities.

Figure 2.4 provides an assessment of the model's forecast uncertainty. The top row of Figure 2.4 records the model's fit over the last

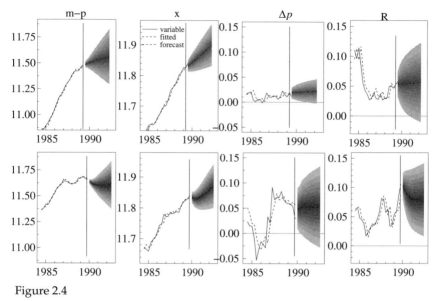

Figure 2.4

Forecasts from the model of UK M1 and forecasts of the artificial series, all with fans depicting forecast uncertainty.

few periods of the estimation sample and the forecasts from that model over the next 12 quarters. "Fan" confidence intervals around the forecasts characterize decreasing probabilities by lighter shades. (Below, we comment on the second row of Figure 2.4.) The forecasts show steady growth in real money and expenditure, along with relatively constant, low levels of inflation and interest rates. If the model is a good specification, the confidence bands should include the outcomes 95% of the time. Because the forecast uncertainty is increasing, the bands are wider, the further ahead the forecast. For some trending variables like output, the confidence intervals continue to widen indefinitely, whereas the confidence intervals for stationary series tend to an asymptote.

Simulations proceed in the following manner. Given the initial conditions of this system and given the estimated values of all its parameters, we now create a replica of the model on a computer. We replace the empirical residuals by pseudo-random numbers with the distributions shown in Figure 2.3. From those pseudo-random numbers, we

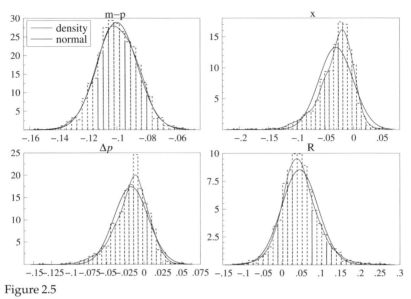

Figure 2.5

Densities of four estimated coefficients from the model of the artificial data.

can construct artificial data from the model, and then re-compute the model's parameter estimates, tests, forecasts, and policy implications. This exercise (or simulation) can be repeated many times, thereby producing sampling distributions of the relevant statistics. For instance, we can simulate how often a test for independent residuals would reject that hypothesis when the errors are in fact independent. Figure 2.5 records the four densities of the estimated disequilibrium feedback coefficients in the system's equations, where those densities are generated by 1000 replications of the artificial data. The coefficient in the real money equation is for the excess demand for money, whereas the remaining densities are for the excess demand for goods in each of the other three equations. Figure 2.5 reveals some departures from normality, but the means of the distributions are close to the empirical estimates.

Returning to Figure 2.4, the lower row in that figure shows the corresponding forecasts and confidence measures for one replication of data generated by our facsimile model. The computer-generated data have properties similar to those of the actual outcomes, as the graphs reveal by the close correspondence between the properties of the forecasts produced empirically and the properties of the forecasts from the artificial computer-generated data, although the latter does over-estimate the variance of inflation.[5] We conclude that by such computer-intensive means, and related analytic studies, we can ascertain the properties of our empirical forecast procedures.

2.9 The Main Problems Affecting Economic Forecasts

With these tools in hand, we now discuss some of the main problems in economic forecasting. In Section 2.3, we discussed a number of possible problems for forecasting, and we encountered the greatest difficulty— that the future is uncertain in ways that we do not yet know. Empirically, the worst shifts appear to be those in the underlying mean of the process, of the form shown in Figure 2.1. Unanticipated shifts in the time series being forecast can lead to substantial discrepancies between forecasts and outcomes, with potentially large policy costs.

Fortunately, not all uncertainties are as disastrous: some shifts are even quite difficult to detect. And, as noted earlier, many possible problems have less pernicious effects when no shifts occur. These problems include having inaccurate data, using an incorrect model, and having poor estimates of its parameters. Although these mistakes worsen forecasts relative to the optimum, they do not by themselves lead to forecast failure. However, when these problems interact with unanticipated shifts, they can exacerbate forecast failure. For example, the preliminary data used at the forecast origin may be much less accurate than the finally revised numbers for that date. In conjunction with a structural break, that data inaccuracy can induce forecast failure.

Another class of problem is that some economic variables appear to be almost inherently unpredictable. Examples include changes in stock-market prices and in currency exchange rates, where foreknowledge of a price change would lead to massive transactions, which

---

[5] That said, the empirical econometric model would have generated a large forecast error in the third quarter of 1989. In that quarter, the Abbey National Building Society demutualized and converted to a commercial bank, greatly increasing M1 as then measured, since measured M1 included current accounts in commercial banks but not those in building societies. While this unanticipated change by Abbey National thus would have generated a large forecast error, it would have had no immediate importance to policy, since nothing had really altered. Shortly following Abbey National's action, the Bank of England discontinued measuring interest-bearing M1.

themselves would usually result in a different outcome. Measures of economic crises form a related class of variables: were crises predictable, action might be taken to offset them so they would then not occur, leading to apparent forecast failure! This type of situation arises in everyday life. A garage mechanic may advise changing a car's brake pads because she "forecasts" that they will shortly fail; but, because she installs new pads, the failure does not occur. That said, few drivers blame their mechanic for a bad forecast, even though some drivers undoubtedly paid unnecessarily for new brake pads.

A closely related issue arises with the bandwagon effect, whereby a forecast's announcement influences the behavior of those concerned. This was first discussed by Morgenstern (1928) and countered by Marget (1929). Provided that the response to the announcement varies continuously as the announcement alters, such a bandwagon effect could in principle be incorporated into the forecast. In the United Kingdom, the Spring of 1968 provides a classic example of the failure to allow for such a reaction. A possible increase in sales tax was announced one quarter ahead of the proposed and eventual increase, leading to an "unanticipated" boom (and then bust) in retail sales.

One additional difficulty in forecasting is that small changes can have large effects. For example, the UK Banking Act of 1984 permitted commercial banks to pay interest on checking accounts, provided that they deducted income tax on that interest at the source. When the Act took effect, competition between the banks for deposits led to high interest rates being offered on such accounts. The corresponding measure of money (i.e., M1) exploded, increasing by more than 50% over the three years 1985–1987. While such responses are sometimes thought to entail nonlinear relations—and may do so in reality—the forecasting problem was predicting the banks' response of raising interest rates so dramatically. Given the high interest rates then offered on checking accounts, the ensuing monetary expansion is actually consistent with previous evidence from linear models.

2.10   Forecasting 300 Years of UK Industrial Output

To illustrate at a practical level some of the difficulties in economic forecasting, this section analyzes UK industrial output over the last three

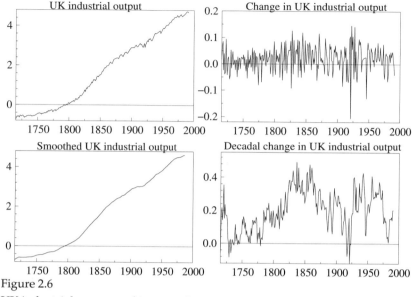

Figure 2.6

UK industrial output and its growth rate, 1715–1991.

centuries. Historically, growth rates of output have altered dramatically, so we consider the plight of a mythical, long-lived economist who is given the task of forecasting UK industrial output over each half-century starting in 1750.

Figure 2.6a records the logarithm of UK industrial output (denoted y) over 1715–1991.[6] The time series of the log-level is manifestly non-stationary, noting that its mean changes greatly over time. The changes (i.e., first differences) in Figure 2.6b highlight that industrial output has grown dramatically but rather unevenly. *Per capita* figures lower the average growth rate somewhat. To smooth the visual appearance, Figure 2.6c reports a decade-long centered moving average of the series. Figure 2.6d plots the decadal changes in that moving average and emphasizes the epochal nature of industrial growth. The series's growth rate declines after an initial short spurt. Growth then exhibits a cyclical pattern until around 1775, after which growth is sustained at about 15%

---

[6]The data were kindly provided by Charlie Bean. The variable Y is "Output in Industry" as compiled from Crafts and Harley (1992, p. 725), Mitchell (1988, p. 846), and the Central Statistical Office (1993). The data were missing during the Second World War, so they were linearly interpolated between 1938 and 1946.

Table 2.1
Means and standard deviations (in %) of Δy_t and $\Delta^2 y_t$.

Statistic	Sample period						
	1715 –1750	1751 –1800	1801 –1850	1851 –1900	1901 –1950	1951 –1991	**1715 –1991**
				Δy			
Mean	0.86	1.07	2.86	2.77	1.95	1.96	**1.96**
SD	3.58	3.47	5.03	4.09	6.32	3.40	**4.54**
				$\Delta^2 y$			
Mean	0.20	–0.09	0.02	0.00	0.11	–0.23	**0.00**
SD	5.32	5.57	8.01	5.02	9.35	4.29	**6.56**

per decade, with a further substantial increase in the rate of growth around 1825, persisting for nearly half a century. Around 1875, the growth rate falls, coinciding with the onset of the "great depression", during which the price level fell for almost 20 years. The crash of 1919–1921 is highly visible, whereas the 1929–1935 depression is not obvious: the United Kingdom was much less affected by that Great Depression than the United States. Finally, the postwar boom is marked, as is the downturn engineered in 1979–1982.

To illustrate the large changes that have occurred, Table 2.1 records the means and standard deviations (SD) of the annual growth rate of output Δy_t (where $\Delta y_t = y_t - y_{t-1}$) and the change in that growth rate $\Delta^2 y_t$ (where $\Delta^2 y_t = \Delta y_t - \Delta y_{t-1}$). The table reports these measures over 50-year subsamples and over the full sample. Across different subsamples, mean growth rates differ by a factor of three and standard deviations by a factor of nearly two. To illustrate the "regular uncertainty" noted at the end of Section 2.2, Figure 2.7 plots the histograms and densities of the growth rate and its change (i.e., the acceleration in output) over 1715–1825 and over the whole sample. These graphs show important changes in the distributions over time; the normal distribution appears for comparison. Overall, acceleration was zero.

By itself, non-stationarity in the level of output is not necessarily problematic, since we could remove both deterministic and stochastic

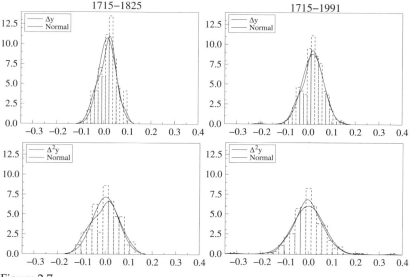

Figure 2.7

Densities of the growth and acceleration in UK industrial output, 1715–1825 and 1715–1991.

trends by differencing and then analyze growth rates. However, the growth rate itself changed greatly, and those changes would have been harder to forecast. Few writers at the time foresaw the consequences of the burgeoning Industrial Revolution until it was well under way; and many of the most vocal writers focused on the Industrial Revolution's drawbacks by creating "dark Satanic mills", rather than on its benefits from starting a prolonged upswing in general living standards. Nevertheless, we will pretend to "forecast" industrial output up to 50 years ahead, using models based on the preceding (typically) 50-year period. We thus have forecasts for 1751–1800, 1801–1850, 1851–1900, 1901–1950, and 1951–1991.

Three simple models are used for constructing the forecasts. The first model is a linear trend model of output. The second is a "constant change" model. The third is a no-acceleration model, which generates a forecast equivalent to "the student is still standing at the bus stop" in our analogy. If the world were non-stochastic, these models would all be identical. However, they behave differently in stochastic worlds,

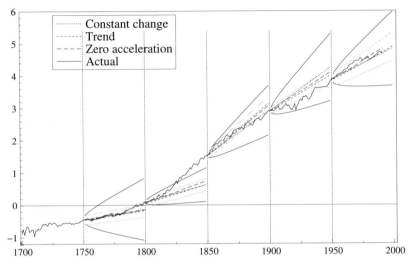

Figure 2.8

Forecasts of UK industrial output over successive 50-year horizons.

due to different treatments of their unexplained components. If the underlying growth rate were constant, all three would deliver unbiased forecasts, and they would differ mainly in the anticipated and actual precision of the forecasts. If the growth rate were to change, the three forecasts could differ markedly. By its construction, the third forecast is not likely to be reliable beyond the very short term, so it may well perform badly on the long horizons considered here.[7]

Figure 2.8 records the three sets of forecasts for successive 50-year horizons, with corresponding forecast confidence intervals for each set of forecasts. To provide some "smoothness" in the no-acceleration forecast, that forecast is based on the average growth over five decades available for estimation. That is, for a forecast h periods ahead with estimation sample ending in period T, that forecast is $\Delta_1 \widehat{y}_{T+h}$ $(= \widehat{y}_{T+h} - \widehat{y}_{T+h-1})$ and is set equal to $0.02\Delta_{50}y_T$ $(= (y_T - y_{T-50})/50)$.

---

[7] A more full-blown econometric model might explain industrial output by demand and supply factors, such as incomes, the price of food relative to other goods, and the quantities of labor, capital, and other inputs. In turn, these variables would need to be modeled. The illustration here only considers scalar models of industrial output, forecasting it by its past behavior: Section 2.8 described how to forecast from an econometric model.

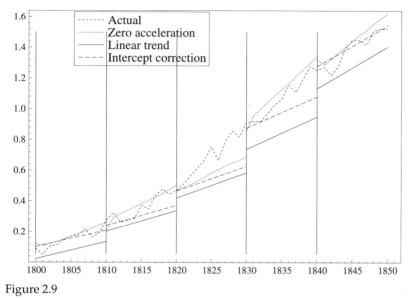

Figure 2.9
Zero-acceleration and constant-trend forecasts over 10-year horizons, 1801–1850.

A given set of confidence intervals should include the outcomes 95% of the time if the confidence intervals were correctly computed, and were computed under the correct assumptions. The trend forecast and its error bands are given by solid lines; the constant-growth forecast and its error bands are given by dotted lines; and the zero-acceleration forecast is shown as a dashed line, but without a confidence interval, which would otherwise swamp the scale. All three forecasts appear very similar, even over long horizons. In almost every 50-year period, some of the realizations lie outside the confidence intervals for the trend forecasts, and sometimes very significantly so, as in the second period (1801–1850). This exemplifies forecast failure of that model. We are not surprised that that model mis-forecasts the Industrial Revolution: the source of this forecast failure is the changed trend rate of growth. The constant-growth model also fails for that episode, and almost everywhere it has a greater forecast uncertainty than does the trend model.

To highlight the distinct behavior of the constant-trend and zero-acceleration forecasts, Figure 2.9 shows those forecasts over successive

10-year horizons for 1801–1850. The constant-trend forecast is a solid line and is based on the preceding 50 observations. The no-acceleration forecast is a dashed line and is based on $0.1\Delta_{10}y_T$. (Below, we comment on the dotted line.) The outcomes illustrate the much better perform-ance of the no-acceleration model on shorter horizons: the contrast in forecasts is particularly stark after 1830. The new theory of forecasting correctly predicts which of these forecasting methods will win, assum-ing that the Industrial Revolution induced shifts in the models' determ-inistic components. The adaptive, no-acceleration method avoids the systematic failure of the constant-trend model.

2.11 Some Potential Solutions

The example above is deliberately contrived to illustrate several po-tential solutions to forecasting when a data process is non-stationary. First, specifying the model in the differences of the variables removes the intercept term, and transforms step shifts to "blips". Nothing can prevent forecast failure if there is an unanticipated break; but once the break is past, some forecasting methods—such as those in differences—are much more robust than others, such as those in levels. Just as first differencing removes the intercept, second differencing removes a lin-ear trend. Second differencing consequently reduces shifts in the *growth rate* to blips.

Second, updating estimates helps the model adapt to changing be-havior in the data. Linear-trend forecasts based on estimates from only the previous 10 data points are much more accurate here, despite the resulting decrease in the precision of the estimated coefficients.

Third, when the first of a sequence of forecasts is in error, the re-maining forecasts often suffer similarly. Consequently, an "intercept shift", equal to the last observed error, can considerably improve fore-cast performance, as shown by the dotted line in Figure 2.9. Every fore-cast is much improved, sometimes sufficiently to "win". To succeed in forecasting competitions, econometric models need to mimic the adapt-ability of the best forecasting devices, while retaining their foundations in economic analysis. Intercept corrections provide one route towards their achieving both aims.

2.12 Conclusions

A forecast is a statement about a future event. This chapter initially examined various forecasting methods used by economists, and it showed that there typically is no unique measure for evaluating and ranking forecasts. A comparison of empirical and artificial data then illustrated how a new theoretical framework helps interpret the results from economic forecasting.

As the analysis of UK industrial output demonstrated, the main problem confronting successful economic forecasting appears to be the inherent non-stationarity of economic data. When the future does not look like the past and present, forecasting requires more than extrapolation. While economic forecasts from econometric systems have a poor historical track record and face many potential and real problems, the recently extended theory of economic forecasting offers a vehicle for understanding and learning from failures, and for consolidating our growing knowledge of economic behavior. Consequently, despite their present travails, econometric systems provide the best long-run hope for successful economic forecasting, especially as suitable methods are developed to improve their robustness to unanticipated breaks.

Acknowledgments

The research underlying this chapter was generously financed by the UK Economic and Social Research Council over many years, and I am pleased to acknowledge my gratitude for their support through the funding of *The Econometrics of Macroeconomic Forecasting* (grant L116251015). Financial support from the Leverhulme Trust for a Personal Research Professorship is also gratefully acknowledged. All the computations and graphics were performed in the PcGive Professional suite of econometric programs; see Doornik and Hendry (2001a), Doornik and Hendry (2001b), and Hendry and Doornik (2001). I am delighted to thank Mike Clements, Neil Ericsson, Vivien Hendry, Hans-Martin Krolzig, Michael Massmann, Grayham Mizon, Adrian Pagan, and the Economics Research Team at Dun and Bradstreet for their many helpful comments.

3 Economic Modeling for Fun and Profit

Paul Turner

Summary

This chapter considers the role of economics in models for generating economic forecasts. We discuss the advantages that a model based on economic theory has relative to a pure time-series model, illustrating their differences with forecasts of the UK's Gross Domestic Product. In economic forecasting, the primary benefits of a more fully specified economic model arise when analyzing economic policy. For instance, the government may adjust policy variables such as the interest rate and tax rates, which themselves affect the course of the economy. Policy shifts thus can alter economic forecasts, provided that the forecasting model incorporates the policy variables. We develop a simple but fully articulated model of the UK economy to illustrate how to generate forecasts under different policy regimes.

3.1 Introduction

In Chapter 2, David Hendry lists six methods by which economic forecasts can be made. However, only two of these methods exhibit any degree of statistical rigor:

- we can build a purely statistical model based on the past data of the variable in question, and we can then extrapolate that behavior into the future; or

42

- we can build a model based on economic theory and then use our knowledge of the structure of the economy to predict its future behavior.

The first of these methods constitutes a pure time-series approach. The second is often described as a structural approach. In practice, the structural approach is more costly in terms of time and effort, and it is sometimes subject to controversy because economists may disagree about which economic theory to use. Moreover, the forecasts generated by structural economic models are often no "better" than those generated by time-series models, at least when assessed statistically in terms of variability and degree of bias from the actual outcomes. Because structural economic models are so costly and the resulting gains in forecasting accuracy are likely to be small, the question naturally arises as to why anyone would adopt a structural modeling approach rather than a time-series approach.

In fact, a structural modeling approach has numerous advantages. These advantages arise because a simple time-series forecast is rarely enough to satisfy a client, whether that client is a government minister, a business executive, or a journal editor. The forecaster always needs to be ready to answer follow-up questions. While the structural modeler is usually well-equipped to do this, the time-series modeler can often be left struggling for an answer.

For example, let's ask our forecasters to prepare forecasts of the sales volume for a corporation. Suppose that both the structural modeler and the time-series forecaster generate sets of forecasts implying that sales will fall drastically in the coming year. The company chairman is alarmed by this and so decides to cut prices and increase the advertising budget to counteract the fall in sales. The chairman now turns to the forecasters and asks how these changes affect their forecasts. Our structural modeler taps in a few changes on his or her laptop and immediately produces a new set of figures. By contrast, the time-series forecaster can only reply that there is no change to the forecasts because the time-series forecasts aren't affected by such factors in the first place.

In this chapter, we discuss in greater detail some of the advantages that a structural modeling approach can offer to forecasting. Section 3.2 illustrates the advantages by constructing time-series and structural forecasts of the UK's Gross Domestic Product. Section 3.3 develops a simple but fully articulated model of the UK economy, and we show how it can be used to evaluate the economy's behavior and to generate forecasts under alternative policy regimes. Section 3.4 concludes.

3.2 Alternative Forecasting Methods

Let us begin by considering a simple example, which will allow us to compare the two alternative forecasting methods. Suppose we wish to forecast future Gross Domestic Product (or GDP)—the total output of the economy. One approach is to build a time-series model of GDP. While there may be better time-series models of GDP, a good candidate arises from modeling the log of GDP as a random walk with drift:

$$y_t = y_{t-1} + \alpha + u_t, \tag{3.1}$$

where y is the log of GDP, α is the drift, u is an error term, and t is the time index. Equation (3.1) models current output y_t as equal to its past value y_{t-1}, plus a percentage drift α, plus an error u_t. That is, output grows at a constant rate on average, but output's actual growth rate fluctuates randomly from period to period.

This random-walk model fits the data well and provides forecasts that act as a benchmark for other more complex forecasting procedures. If we estimate this model using annual UK data for the period 1970–1997, we obtain the following result:

$$\Delta y_t \quad = \quad \underset{(4.68)}{0.0202} \tag{3.2}$$

$$DW = 1.49 \qquad\qquad LM(2) = 2.27\ (0.13)$$
$$ARCH(1) = 0.77\ (0.39) \qquad NORM = 0.11\ (0.94),$$

where Δy_t is the first difference of the log of GDP (i.e., $\Delta y_t = y_t - y_{t-1}$). Hence, equation (3.2) represents a re-arrangement of (3.3), with α estimated as 0.0202. The value in parentheses below the coefficient α is the t-ratio for testing whether α is significantly different from zero. DW is the Durbin–Watson statistic for testing for residual autocorrelation, $LM(2)$ is the F-form of the Lagrange Multiplier test statistic for second-order serial correlation in the residuals, $ARCH(1)$ is the F-form of the Lagrange multiplier test statistic for first-order autoregressive conditional heteroscedasticity in the residuals, and NORM is the Jarque–Bera test statistic for normality of the residuals. Probability values are given in parentheses next to the diagnostic test statistics: see Durbin and Watson (1950), Durbin and Watson (1951), Godfrey (1978), Engle (1982), and Jarque and Bera (1980) respectively for details, and Kiviet (1986) for a justification of the F-form. None of these tests rejects the null of "well-behaved" residuals.

The constant term α, or drift parameter, shows that the average annual rate of growth for GDP for this sample is just over 2% per annum. Given this growth rate, along with some starting value for GDP, we can easily calculate forecasts for GDP over any time horizon. However, the expected variance of the actual outcome around the predicted path will increase as the forecast horizon extends into the future; see Chapter 5. Moreover, as Chapter 2 discusses, variables such as GDP often exhibit "structural breaks" that are not easily captured by simple time-series models.

The structural modeling approach is considerably more complex than the time-series approach. We can think of it as consisting of the following stages.

- We first decide on an appropriate theoretical structure for the economy. Among other things, this requires distinguishing exogenous variables (those determined outside the model) from endogenous variables (those determined within the model).
- We express this structure in mathematical form.
- We then use data to assign numerical values to the parameters of the theoretical model.
- If some variables are exogenous to the model, those variables need to be forecast, e.g., using time-series methods.
- Conditional on those forecasts of the exogenous variables, we use our model to generate forecasts of the endogenous variables.

This is a more involved process than that for generating time-series forecasts. However, there are two advantages to the structural approach. First, the economic theory used in setting up the model can help improve the accuracy of the forecasts by adding extra information to the model. Second, the structural approach enables us to conduct simulations under different scenarios for the future state of the economy. Calculations below illustrate the second advantage in particular.

Table 3.1
Comparison of GDP forecasts from time-series and structural models (£1000 million at 1990 prices).

Year	Time-series	Structural	Structural	Structural
		Assumption about world trade growth		
	Anything	5% growth	8% growth	11% growth
1998	548.4	542.5	551.1	560.2
1999	559.5	552.8	562.3	572.6
2000	570.8	565.3	575.9	587.5

In Table 3.1, we contrast the forecasts generated by our time-series model with those generated by a small structural model. In each case, the forecast has been made using data through 1997. The time-series forecasts are based on the constant growth-rate model estimated in (3.2), in which GDP grows at a rate of 2.02% on average. Forecasts from the structural model are derived from SIMPLE, a small macroeconomic model consisting of 13 behavioral equations and a number of accounting identities.

Table 3.1 emphasizes the conditional nature of the structural forecasts. To use such a model, we must make assumptions about the future behavior of the exogenous variables. In Table 3.1, we have made three alternative assumptions about the growth rate of world trade over the forecasting horizon. These alternative assumptions correspond to "pessimistic", "neutral", and "optimistic" scenarios, as represented by assumed world trade growth rates of 5%, 8%, and 11% respectively. The assumption about world trade affects the structural model's GDP forecasts in a qualitatively predictable way, with the growth rate of GDP increasing with that of world trade. The conditional nature of these forecasts makes them more difficult to construct than the time-series forecasts, but it also entails possible uses for the structural model that are simply not available in the univariate time-series approach.

President Reagan is once said to have requested a "one-armed economist" on the grounds that his economic advisors always qualified their forecasts with the phrase "on the other hand". Still, the two-handed approach often may be more appropriate. Forecasts are necessarily conditional on a set of assumptions about the future. These assumptions should be recognized when the forecasts are constructed, and they should be stated clearly when the forecasts are presented. So, although time-series forecasts are quick and easy to compute, a structural approach has significant advantages by being able to cope with a variety of different scenarios.

3.3   A Basic Model of the UK Economy

In this section, we examine another use for structural models—the analysis of the economy's behavior under alternative policy regimes. Such analysis is important for the forecaster if he or she expects a change in policy regime during the forecast period.

To investigate the effects of policy changes, we first set out a basic model of the UK economy with the following four features.

- The long-run growth path of the economy is driven by supply-side factors—in particular, the growth in the supply and productivity of the factors of production.
- In the short run, aggregate demand affects real output. In the longer run, prices rise if output increases above its capacity value, where the latter is determined by the supply side of the economy.
- The model incorporates financial markets through the effects of the interest rate on investment and through linkages between interest rates, the exchange rate, and aggregate demand.
- Expectations are determined rationally. That is, they are consistent with the predictions of the model.

These principles are embodied in the following basic model, where y_t denotes constant-price GDP with y_t^* as capacity output, i_t and i_t^f the domestic and foreign nominal interest rates, π_t and π_t^c domestic inflation and core inflation, e_t the nominal exchange rate (foreign currency units per £), p_t and p_t^f domestic and foreign prices, m_t the nominal money stock, and the superscript ^{e} denotes a rational expectation:

Aggregate demand

$$y_t = y_t^* + \alpha_1 y_{t-1} + \alpha_2 (i_t - \pi_t^c)$$
$$+ \alpha_3 (e_t + p_t - p_t^f) \tag{3.3}$$

Demand for money

$$m_t - p_t = \beta_1 y_t + \beta_2 i_t \tag{3.4}$$

Inflation

$$\pi_t = \pi_t^c + \gamma (y_t - y_t^*) \tag{3.5}$$

Core inflation

$$\pi_t^c = \delta \pi_{t-1} + (1 - \delta) \pi_{t+1}^e \tag{3.6}$$

Interest rate parity

$$i_t - i_t^f = e_t - e_{t+1}^e \tag{3.7}$$

Growth in output capacity

$$y_t^* = \phi + y_{t-1}^* . \tag{3.8}$$

This formulation is based on the Dornbusch (1976) model, as it combines sticky goods prices with flexible asset prices. Price inflation is partly backward-looking and partly forward-looking, following the overlapping contracts literature associated with Taylor (1979) and Calvo (1983). Batini and Haldane (1999a, 1999b) have recently used similar models at the Bank of England to provide a stylized account of the UK economy's behavior. Bean (1998) also estimates a similar model and uses it to analyze recent UK monetary policy, although his model lacks the open-economy aspects of the model above.

The assumption of rational expectations helps defend the model in (3.3)–(3.8) against the Lucas (1976) critique, which states that, unless expectations are modeled correctly, the model's assumed parameter values will change if the policy regime changes. However, the inclusion of rational expectations creates a problem when solving the model, because it includes two forward-looking variables: the expectations of inflation and the exchange rate, both one period ahead (π_{t+1}^e and e_{t+1}^e). In practice, we allow for these variables by adopting the Fair–Taylor solution method, in which we solve the model conditional on an assumed path for the expectational variables and then iterate over this path until it converges with the model solution.

The α_i parameters are estimated using a small empirical model. All the other parameters are imposed. The parameter values used to simulate this model are as follows:

$$
\begin{aligned}
\alpha_1 &= 0.69 \\
\alpha_2 &= -0.38 \\
\alpha_3 &= -0.12 \\
\beta_1 &= 1.0 \\
\beta_2 &= -0.5 \\
\gamma &= 0.7 \\
\delta &= 0.5 \\
\phi &= 0.025 .
\end{aligned}
\tag{3.9}
$$

The choice of the parameter δ is crucial for the model simulations, as δ determines the degree to which inflation is forward-looking. To illustrate this, Figures 3.1 and 3.2 present alternative time paths for output and inflation during a period of disinflation, with the policymaker attempting to bring inflation down from an actual rate of 5% to a target rate of 2.5%. In the backward-looking simulations, the parameter δ is set to unity, i.e., core inflation is purely backward-looking. For the forward-looking case, we adopt a mixed approach: δ is set to 0.5, meaning that core inflation is partly backward-looking and partly forward-looking. In both scenarios, we fix the money growth rate at 5%, equal to the sum of the growth rate for real output and the target inflation rate. As these simulations show, forward-looking expectations make a substantial difference to the economy's behavior. In particular, inflation falls faster and the output cost is much lower when expectations are partly forward-looking rather purely backward-looking.

The facility to conduct simulations under alternative assumptions about forward-looking behavior is, in itself, a valuable feature of a model-based approach. Policymakers need to be informed about the range of possible outcomes for the economy. If there is uncertainty about the extent to which agents are forward-looking, then a range of simulations may be required to assess the likely effects of economic policy.

We now move on to illustrate the value of model-based simulations in a current policy debate. A low and stable rate of inflation is widely accepted as a desirable target for government economic policy. However, debate continues as to how this can best be achieved. During the 1970s and early 1980s, some governments, including that of the United Kingdom, followed the proposal of Milton Friedman (1960), who advocated using the money supply as an intermediate target. By

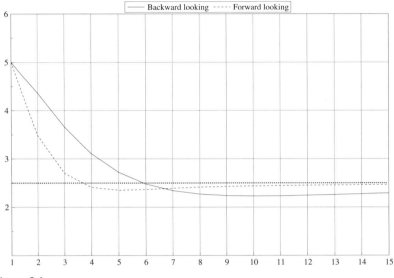

Figure 3.1
Disinflation with backward-looking and partly forward-looking expectations
(% change in prices).

stabilizing the growth rate of the money supply, governments would
then stabilize the rate of inflation. However, in recent years, the emphasis has switched to direct targeting of the inflation rate. Taylor
(1993) has argued that the central bank should adjust the interest rate
so as to target inflation. Many central banks now operate a form of
"Taylor rule", in which interest rates are adjusted up or down in order
to bring inflation into line with its targeted value.

Because the extent of forward-looking inflation expectations is crucial in determining the economy's response to such policy rules, we
need to give some thought to the value of the parameter δ. Considerable literature evaluates the effects of overlapping contracts: see Taylor
(1979) and Calvo (1983), the latter of whom indicates that this parameter will not take the extreme values 0 or 1, but will lie somewhere in
between. However, we might also expect the Lucas critique to apply to
this sort of parameter. Because the policy regime in force may affect the
extent to which individuals are forward-looking about core inflation,
estimation of δ based on historical data may not generate a value of δ

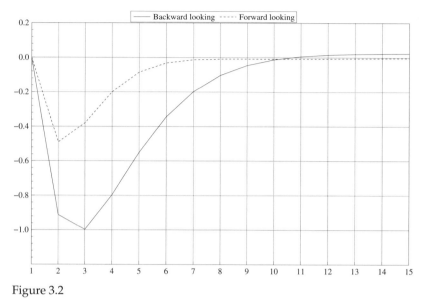

Figure 3.2
Output cost of disinflation with backward-looking and partly forward-looking expectations (% deviation of output from capacity).

suitable for subsequent policy analysis. Thus, we simply fix δ at 0.5, to reflect our assumption that core inflation is partly backward-looking and partly forward-looking.

Having discussed the importance of forward-looking behavior, we can now use our model to simulate the effects of the alternative policy regimes on the disinflation process. Figures 3.3 and 3.4 plot the projected paths of inflation and output under Friedman's fixed percentage-rate money-targeting rule and under the Taylor rule.

First, consider the behavior of inflation itself. From Figure 3.3, both policies eventually succeed in achieving the target, but the Friedman rule undershoots by 0.5% in Year 4 and overshoots slightly around Year 8. The Taylor rule generates considerably smoother adjustment, although at a slightly slower rate.

Second, consider the behavior of output. As Figure 3.4 shows, both policies generate short-term recessions, but with differing adjustment paths. The recession under the Taylor rule is quicker to occur and quicker to disappear. Output under the Friedman rule tends to cycle, with output rising above capacity in Years 6–8.

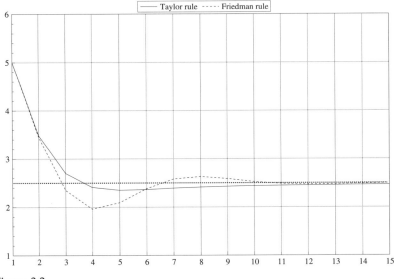

Figure 3.3
Disinflation paths with a Taylor interest-rate rule and a Friedman monetary rule (% change in prices).

It is hard to judge the alternative policies from these diagrams alone. However, the Taylor rule does appear to generate smoother paths for the economy than does the Friedman rule. One reason may be that the Taylor rule targets inflation directly, rather indirectly, as through an intermediate money-supply target.

3.4   Concluding Remarks

In this chapter, we have discussed some ways in which a structural modeling approach can help in the production and use of economic forecasts. This approach is advantageous, mainly because a forecast by itself is almost never enough. Users of economic forecasts often require simulations under alternative scenarios, which in turn require a fully-articulated model rather than a simplified time-series model. The structural modeling approach also enables simulating the effects of alternative policy regimes on the variables of interest.

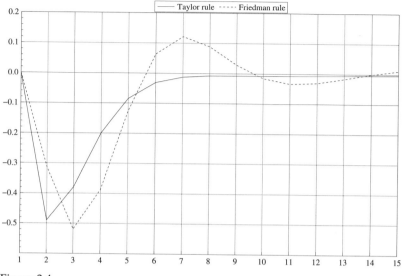

Figure 3.4
Output cost of disinflation with a Taylor interest-rate rule and a Friedman monetary rule (% deviation of output from capacity).

Acknowledgments

This paper was originally given as an address to sixth-form (final-year High School) students of economics.

4 Making Sense of Published Economic Forecasts

Diane Coyle

Summary

For some time, the author has given the Golden Guru award to the year's best forecaster of the UK "misery index", which is an index depending upon UK inflation, unemployment, and economic growth. Historically, forecasters have herded together on these three key measures, with the Golden Guru award being won by only a narrow margin and with very few repeat winners. Forecasters face a difficult task; and journalists could improve their own presentations of forecasts, as by avoiding spurious precision and by explaining the uncertainties involved in forecasting. Additional complications arise with forecasts used in the conduct of economic policy.

4.1 A Famous Forecasting Competition

The most coveted prize in British economic forecasting is *The Independent* newspaper's **Golden Guru** statue. Each year, I compile a table of the best economic forecasts published in the Treasury's monthly summary. These forecasts are mostly produced by City economists (i.e., London financial analysts), whose degree of sophistication varies widely. Some forecasts are also from standard large macroeconometric models. I'm thus comparing some forecasts that are little more than rules of thumb or hunches—perhaps satisfying certain national accounting identities—to others based on years of research and the pooled expertise of some of the country's leading economists.

Over the years, all sorts have won. The latest three winners have been the economics team at the Salomon Brothers investment bank, a lone economist at Hermes Pension Fund Management, and the National Institute of Economic and Social Research; see Chapter 9 on the last. The contest tends to exclude official bodies, partly because they don't publish forecasts for all the relevant variables, and partly because they may make conventional assumptions. For instance, Her Majesty's Treasury assumes unemployment constant or makes a conditional projection, and the Bank of England assumes a constant short-term nominal interest rate.

The winner is determined by the minimum sum of squared errors for one year ahead on three forecast variables:

- the target inflation rate in the final quarter of the year, which is constructed from the retail price index;
- the claimant-count unemployment rate, also in the final quarter; and
- the full-year growth rate of the Gross Domestic Product (GDP).

The rationale for this choice is a mix of policy relevance and simplicity. After all, readers and citizens care about inflation, jobs, and income growth, so this isn't a bad metric. That said, it is not a very good way of assessing the quality of economic forecasting, either.

The forecasts are all made at slightly different times, using different data sets. Those published in January summarize forecasts made between November and early January. I am even told that some organizations changed the date of their forecasting cycle to have a better stab at winning the prized Golden Guru statue.

A few additional notes on the data are also relevant. The retail price index (RPI) and the claimant-count data are never revised, but data on GDP certainly are. My calculations use the first estimate of GDP for the full year, and these preliminary numbers are sometimes revised dramatically. For example, GDP growth for 1998 was initially estimated in January 1999 at 2.5%. In February, it was revised down to 2.4%, and in April downward again to 2.1%. In July, it was revised back up to 2.2%. If this last estimate had been the original number, the winner would have been somebody else, somebody who was actually in the middle of the pack.

There are two points that follow from this finding. The first point concerns the behavior of the forecasters: forecasters herd together. There is actually very little distinction between them on these three key measures, although obviously a much wider distribution of forecasts exists on variables that are themselves the difference between two big numbers, such as the balance of payments or the Public Sector Borrowing Requirement (PSBR). In part because of the herd behavior, the Golden Guru is only ever won by a narrow margin, and the average of all forecasts is itself always ranked in the top few positions. Additionally, there are very few repeat winners, as almost everybody is making an almost identical forecast. Because the GDP data are revised, sometimes substantially, basing the calculations on the first estimate of GDP is a bit like pulling a name out of a crowded hat.

That said, herding is a good strategy for somebody who wants to win the prize. Those economists who are driven by a non-consensus view about how the economy works, or who make forecasts at one extreme or the other, never win. In fact, they are always near the bottom, having always made a big error on at least one of the three variables. For the Golden Guru award, it is better to be a bit wrong on all three counts than absolutely right on two but wildly astray on the third.

The second point is that forecasting involves uncertainty. Part of that uncertainty is not knowing what has happened, even long after the event. We don't know the true structure of the economy, the true values of parameters in econometric models, or the exact shocks that hit the economy; and we may never obtain accurate data measurements either.

Forecasters have sometimes described their task as similar to driving in a thick fog using only the rear-view mirror, but I think that is an understatement. To make the metaphor more exact, add misted windows, an unreliable clutch, a blindfold, and handcuffs—not to mention the unsignposted cliff a hundred meters down the road. Thus, I must offer a profound apology for perpetrating in the Golden Guru contest the notion that the difference between 2.2% and 2.5% measured GDP growth in a given year is at all meaningful.

In that light, the remainder of this chapter focuses on five interrelated themes: spurious precision, forecast errors, targets, uncertainty, and forecast difficulties. Section 4.2 examines the media's tendency to spurious precision and the forecasters' potential and actual role in counteracting that tendency. Section 4.3 discusses some political consequences of forecast errors, looking at the United Kingdom during the late 1980s as a case in point. Section 4.4 elucidates some of the complications that governments encounter when publishing statistics and forecasts, as those figures are apt to influence and be influenced by policy. Economic statistics are measured with error, and forecasts are predictions of an uncertain future, so Section 4.5 turns to the importance of recognizing those imprecisions, particularly when policy lags themselves are uncertain. Section 4.6 illustrates some of the practical difficulties of longer-term forecasting, and Section 4.7 concludes.

4.2   Spurious Precision

In the media, spurious precision is very hard to avoid. The importance of being precise is instilled in Journalism College, and for good reason. Apart from anything else, precision signals that the reporter has a hinterland of knowledge going beyond the reporter's relatively few words that make it to the printed page or on the airwaves.

In many instances, precision is absolutely proper. It can be misleading, however, where there is actually some underlying uncertainty. This is as true of much medical and scientific research as of economic forecasting, and we in the media are a very long way from being able to convey uncertainty.

Indeed, *The Independent* is not unusual in its having a computer system that will not allow journalists to write "$2\frac{1}{2}\%$" in figures involving a fraction, even if doing so is intended to convey a sense of approximation. It has to be "2.5%" or, at best, "around 2.5%"; and "around" is likely to get subbed out in order to save a line of print. News editors and sub-editors are also allergic to words such as "probably", "might", and "approximately". If it's only worth a "might", it probably isn't a story.

In addition, reporters are encouraged to talk about share prices "nose-diving" or in "free fall" when they decline by even 1%–2%. That currently corresponds to about 60–120 points on the FTSE-100 index or 100–200 points on the Dow Jones Industrial Average. In the most recent week for which I checked, the FTSE-100 index moved by that much every day. Likewise, we write about somebody "slashing" their growth forecast from (say) 1.2% to 1.0%. This is not an easy culture in which to introduce notions of probability distributions, variance, and margins of error.

Not that innumerate and unscientific journalists—or even their readers—are entirely to blame for this. At least in economics, it is still fairly unusual to present economic forecasts with a range of uncertainty. The UK Treasury's twice-yearly published forecasts do contain a table giving the average errors in past forecasts of selected variables, but this is never reported in the rush to cover the Budget.

It has been harder for the press to ignore the Bank of England's insistence on the presence of forecast uncertainty. In 1994 in its quarterly *Inflation Report*, the Bank introduced a range around its inflation forecast. The Bank's well-known fan charts date from 1996. Its "rivers of blood" chart shows successive 10 percent confidence intervals in shades of red around the central inflation forecast, and the corresponding "rivers of bile" chart uses shades of green for its GDP forecasts; see Chapters 5 and 8 for examples.

The Bank's key innovation, in terms of presentation, was showing the central projection as a thick splodge of a line with ranges fanning out around it. It left newspaper graphics specialists with little option but to print the ranges rather than the point forecasts, or to leave the chart out altogether, which unfortunately most newspapers do. A Bank press officer once asked me plaintively whether the problem was that our computer system just wasn't up to coping with the number of lines on the chart. The Bank's *Inflation Report* now also contains graphs of the probability distributions corresponding to the fan chart at points in the future, but these have yet to reach the mass audience. Additionally, the Bank has started sending a questionnaire to City economists, asking for the probability distributions around their inflation forecasts: that has many of them scurrying back to their econometrics textbooks.

Another recent innovation has been the presentation of margins of error on some official UK statistics. Figures from the UK Labour Force Survey in the monthly Office of National Statistics (ONS) press release on *Labour Market Statistics* now include an indication of sampling variability. The ONS also keeps the magnitudes of revisions to all series under review, although it publishes only occasional articles on its conclusions.

The diligent reporter has an increasing amount of raw material from which to construct a message about the uncertainty inherent in economic forecasting, but it is an uphill struggle. After all, the typical person finds it impossible to get to grips with relative risks in far more important aspects of life. For example, six children a year in Britain are murdered by strangers, and hundreds a year die from car accidents. Parents' fears—and newspaper coverage—focus far more on the former than the latter.

4.3 Forecast Errors

UK Chancellors of the Exchequer [the highest minister of finance, and a member of the British Cabinet] have been swift to blame some combination of inaccurate data and faulty forecasts for anything that goes wrong in the management of the economy. After all, as Eddie George (Governor of the Bank of England) likes to point out, there are only three kinds of economist: those who can add, and those who can't.

Lord Lawson still bristles at the suggestion that he made policy mistakes as Chancellor of the Exchequer in the late 1980s. Given the information and forecasts available at the time, there was no error, he insists. It is worth examining his account of how economic forecasts contributed to the policy decisions that paved the way for what history has tagged the "Lawson boom" of the late 1980s in the United Kingdom.

In his memoir, Lawson claims that, in the early 1980s, when he was financial secretary to the UK Treasury, he was already arguing in favor of abolishing the obligation to publish short-term economic forecasts at Budget time and in the autumn. He notes that Alan Budd, later the UK Treasury's chief economic adviser, favored using private forecasts, observing that even the US Treasury did not prepare its own forecasts of the US economy. Lawson writes:

> He [Alan Budd] pointed out *en passant* that the Treasury spent twice as much on forecasting as the LBS [London

Business School] and NIESR [National Institute for Economic and Social Research] put together, so there was plenty of scope for budgetary and staff economies as well. ... But my main argument against the Treasury forecasts was the political burden they imposed. Because they enjoyed the *imprimatur* of the Treasury they were ... invested by the outside world with a spurious authority, not to mention the status of deliberate policy choices.

However, Lawson thought it would be impossible simply to cease publishing the forecasts while continuing to produce them internally.

So long as forecasts of this kind are made by the Treasury, they will leak, and we shall be accused of suppression and worse if we do not publish them.

As it happened, a hostile official—inevitably known as Deep Throat—was leaking the new Government's gloomy economic forecast to the press, which billed the forecast as "suppressed". Lawson's robust defense was that it was the Chancellor's forecast, and he wasn't going to have his name associated with the nonsense being peddled by Treasury economists. He says:

On closer investigation, I found the Treasury forecasters were predicting the worst economic downturn since the Great Slump of 1929–1931. Yet they expected no fall in inflation at all. This was clearly absurd.

Lord Lawson went on to explain that the forecasts should not have been published, even if he had believed in them. Such dismal forecasts would have damaged confidence and generated immense opposition to government policy. He concludes:

To run such risks merely for the sake of a forecast whose margins of error are known to be very large indeed would be absurd. ...

Denis Healey [a previous Chancellor of the Exchequer] used to claim that he wanted to be to the forecasters what the Boston Strangler was to door-to-door salesmen. I [Lawson] wholeheartedly shared the sentiments. ... Perhaps I should have returned to the charge when I became

Chancellor in 1983. But I was lulled by a period of years when the forecasting record was good, as it tends to be when the economy is expanding at trend rates.

The forecasting trap returned with a vengeance when Lord Lawson became Chancellor. While growth had slowed in late 1985, the Chancellor gave a speech in May 1986 predicting a vigorous resumption of growth, claiming that the economy was working better than it used to—thanks to the Government's reforms. His prediction was, he reminisces, greeted with "ill-concealed scepticism". Lawson argued that there was a pause, not a slowdown—and neither event had been forecast by the Treasury, he complains. There was no clear evidence that the pause was over until third quarter GDP figures were published in November 1986. He then modestly concedes:

> I cannot claim to have foreseen the full extent of the boom that began to develop. Moreover I was not helped by the Treasury's economic forecasts, which despite being regularly castigated by the Labour party as ludicrously optimistic, in fact seriously and consistently underestimated the strength of the upturn. ... The outside forecasts underpredicted the boom by an even greater margin than the Treasury did.

In his memoir, Lawson claims that, with hindsight, the weakness of the pound and soaring house prices ought to have signaled a warning. Lawson says—and rightly, I think—that he would have been attacked, had he run a tougher policy. Inflation, however measured, was down to $3\frac{1}{2}\%$ in 1986. Indeed, the headline rate went below $2\frac{1}{2}\%$. Producer price inflation was also at the lowest level in decades. House prices did start to take off, but this followed several years with virtually no increase in real house prices, and at this stage the housing boom seemed confined to central London.

Real interest rates were already high at around 7%, which was the highest since the 1920s and some $2\frac{1}{2}$ points above the G-7 average. Lawson also claims that, in 1988, he introduced a tight budget. Despite tax cuts worth £6.5 billion a year, public spending was falling in real terms. According to OECD figures for cyclically adjusted government deficits, the UK budget did tighten in each year from 1985 to 1989.

But he would, Lawson writes, have tightened monetary policy further if forecasters had warned him of an impending boom.

4.4   Confusing Public-service Forecasts with Targets

I think Lord Lawson was correct to conclude that it is foolish for politicians to stake their credibility on anything with such wide margins of error as economic statistics or economic forecasts. Yet—ultimately out of a sense of accountability to the electorate, I think—that is exactly what they are prone to do.

This tension is visible in many areas of the present government's policy. For example, there is the pledge to cut the National Health Service's waiting lists. In the Soviet Union under central planning, manufacturers of consumer electronic goods were set production targets in terms of weight, so they put bricks inside their radios and TVs. Likewise, UK hospital managers are now said to be rushing through lots of operations for ingrown toenails: that way they can lop large numbers of people off their waiting lists. Such scepticism aside, how is the quality of public services to be improved if there are no measurable targets by which public servants can be assessed? Measurement is essential: it is important to pin down the numbers, but it is hard to see how this can escape becoming a target that distorts behavior. Perhaps one of the criteria for targets needs to be an assessment of likely distortions of this kind.

Something similar has always happened, and always will, with official economic forecasts. We can argue that, for the sake of transparency, it is absolutely right that the Chancellor should publish any forecasts that he makes. After all, it is a fair question to ask: what does the Chancellor think is going to happen to the economy, and on what basis is he setting policy? In just the same way, the Bank of England should reveal its own assessment of the future. Still, such forecasts are bound to be interpreted as targets in some sense, especially because plans for public spending and taxes will depend on (e.g.) the Chancellor getting it more or less right. If the growth forecast is a target, downward revisions in particular become fraught with difficulty.

In the autumn of 1998, when it became clear that the economy had started to slow more than expected, the Chancellor of the Exchequer

Gordon Brown had to revise down his published forecast for 1999 GDP growth. Luckily, he had a good excuse: the global financial crisis. The IMF was also revising down all its growth forecasts, even for the dynamic US economy. Michael Mussa, then the IMF's chief forecaster, said:

> We've been predicting slower US growth for three years now, and we're going to carry on predicting it until the economy gets it right.

A few months later, after the monthly and quarterly data for the United Kingdom had again proved weak—and weaker than most City analysts expected—the Chancellor was under pressure to revise down his GDP growth forecast once again, to below the 1%–1.5% range published in the pre-Budget report. However, Mr. Brown stuck to that range, reasoning that GDP growth of (say) 0.7% was around the same as growth of 1% or even 1.2%. The big picture was unchanged: the economy would slow to a near standstill without going into recession. That was also right. The herd of City forecasters, having trooped down the hill in the early months of 1999, now trooped right back up again. Mr. Brown was correct not to change and correct, also, to publish a forecast *range* for growth. That is one way to convey the public message that there is a margin of error.

4.5 Forecast Uncertainty and Policy Lags

All that said, Mr. Brown also started to untie himself from the stake of economic forecasting when he shifted operational responsibility for half of macroeconomic policy to the Bank of England. The Bank is well aware of that burden. In a recent paper, Mervyn King, the Bank's deputy governor, made the following remarks.

> Perhaps one of the strongest arguments for delegating decisions on interest rates to an independent central bank is that, whereas democratically elected politicians do not often receive praise when they say "I don't know", those words should be ever present on the tongues of central bankers. And, in a state of ignorance, it is important for the central

bank to be transparent about both what it thinks it understands, and what it knows it does not understand.

There is a further problem, though, in the public debate about economic prospects. It is difficult to convey not just inescapable uncertainty and lack of knowledge about the economy's structure, but also
the presence of lags and the need to react to forward-looking indicators,
which may require using policy preemptively. This task is now mainly
the Bank of England's problem, at least as long as we have a Chancellor
who does not believe in active counter-cyclical fiscal policy.

Anybody who has suffered a certain type of shower well appreci-
ates the parallel problems in policy introduced by the long and variable
lags between interest rate changes and inflation outcomes. That shower
is the type without a pump, where the water temperature depends on
the water pressure. Not only is there a delay between turning the taps
and getting a different temperature of water, the delay and the final
temperature vary depending on that day's pressure in the water mains.
That in turn depends on all sorts of other factors, including whether or
not the neighbor is running the washing machine. It is only human to
over-react, turn the tap too far, and then swear when the water comes
out too hot or cold. The combination of uncertainty and impatience is
a difficult one for policymakers.

The Bank's Monetary Policy Committee (MPC) is in charge of the
tap, and it has to get the temperature right for all the rest of us. Not
only will the MPC face complaints if it gets policy wrong, it will also
be criticized for getting policy right. Because of the lags involved, the
MPC ought to start turning the tap before it is readily apparent that
anything *is* wrong.

I think that this explains the intermittent attraction of policy rules,
such as the one associated with early-stage monetarism. A money-
growth target is appealing to the extent that the annual growth rate
of the monetary aggregate M4 is a reliable early-warning indicator of
inflation. Similarly, middle-period Nigel Lawson, writing his memoirs,
had obviously concluded that house-price inflation and the exchange
rate were the best leading indicators. Unfortunately, there is neither an
intellectual consensus nor incontrovertible empirical evidence on what
constitute good leading indicators of inflation. Indeed, the best leading
indicator for inflation is still an economic forecast that takes account of

all of today's possible influences on prices next year and the year after. There seems no escaping it.

4.6   Forecasting Is Difficult

Nobody ever said that forecasting was easy. In June 1998, Paul Krugman, one of the most prominent people in the economics profession today, wrote an article called "Why most economists' predictions are wrong". Krugman was keen to debunk the so-called New Economy view, namely, that we are living in a time of spectacular economic progress driven by new technology. He did so by looking back at how wrong a famous book written in 1967 had been.

Herman Kahn, in his book *The Year 2000*, predicted all sorts of things that did come true in the year 2000. For example, he predicted that most people would have computers at home and that they would be able to use them both to search databases and to communicate. He also predicted mobile phones, VCRs, and home satellite dishes.

Pretty good going. Unfortunately, he also predicted that, over the last third of the century, living standards would double, despite a sharp reduction in work time. He thought that, by 2000, the norm in the United States would be a 30-hour work week with 13 weeks of vacation per year. He then went on to worry about the social implications of excessive leisure time.

He and most other people at the time were overly optimistic about future productivity growth, extrapolating recent performance into the far future. Such growth did not materialize, nor did many other inventions predicted in his book, such as undersea cities and house-cleaning robots. Science fiction novelists seem much better than "experts" at getting this kind of prediction right.

Examples of this kind of extrapolation abound. Not so long ago, it was commonplace to hear people saying that Japan would supplant the United States as the world economic superpower, that the tiger economies would make Asia the most dynamic region in the world, and that Indonesia would become one of the world's biggest economies by 2020.

Despite such cautionary tales, Krugman was persuaded by the magazine publishing his article to give his own economic forecasts. He said productivity would drop sharply in 1998:

> Nineteen ninety-seven, which was a very good year for worker productivity, has led many pundits to conclude that the great technology-led boom has begun. They are wrong. Last year will prove to have been a blip. Inflation will be back. ... In 1999 inflation will probably be more than 3 percent; with only moderate bad luck—say, a drop in the dollar—it could easily top 4 percent. ... Within two or three years, the current mood of American triumphalism—our belief that we have pulled economically and technologically ahead of the rest of the world—will evaporate. ... The growth of the Internet will slow drastically, as the flaw in "Metcalfe's Law"—which states that the number of potential connections in a network is proportional to the square of the number of participants—becomes apparent: most people have nothing to say to each other!

Krugman might be right eventually, perhaps even for next year, but he was wrong for 1999. He broke one of the cardinal rules of forecasting—which is say what, or when, but never both at the same time.

4.7 Conclusions

What are the lessons of experience? I think that there are contrasting lessons for politicians, technocrats, and journalists. For politicians, the message is keep it bland and vague. Avoid figures altogether. Abolish the Treasury forecast, which at best adds no new information about the economy and at worst offers tremendous hostages to fortune. Base the budget calculations on consensus forecasts or conventional assumptions, such as $1\frac{1}{2}\%$–2% growth and $2\frac{1}{2}\%$ inflation. Mr. Brown and his successors could even use the excellent "Be Your Own Chancellor" web site run by the Institute for Fiscal Studies.

For technocrats at the Bank of England, there is no escape from producing growth and inflation forecasts. That said, the optimum approach may involve even greater transparency. Because interest rates are set once a month and most data are monthly, there is a strong case for publishing new forecasts each month as well, perhaps as a footnote to the minutes of the Monetary Policy Committee.

We journalists would get used to the idea that forecasts shift over time with new information. We would also get bored quickly with all the numbers. As I started out by indicating, journalism overlaps with the entertainment industry. Even in reporting economic forecasts, I have to regretfully conclude that we're glamorous but shallow.

Acknowledgments

This chapter was prepared when I was Economics Editor at *The Independent*, and I am grateful to my colleagues there, especially Hamish McRae and Philip Thornton, for many useful discussions.

5 Forecast Uncertainty in Economic Modeling

Neil R. Ericsson

Summary

This chapter provides an introduction to forecast uncertainty in empirical economic modeling. Forecast uncertainty is defined, various measures of forecast uncertainty are examined, and some sources and consequences of forecast uncertainty are analyzed. Empirical illustrations with the US trade balance, UK inflation and real national income, and the US/UK exchange rate help clarify the issues involved.

5.1 Introduction

This chapter considers forecast uncertainty in econometric modeling, analyzing at a general level certain sources of uncertainty present in economic forecasting. Economic forecasts feature prominently in business decision-making, government policy analysis, and economic research. Economic forecasts typically differ from the realized outcomes, with discrepancies between forecasts and outcomes reflecting forecast uncertainty. Depending upon the degree of forecast uncertainty, forecasts may range from being highly informative to being completely useless for the tasks at hand.

Four issues are central to the discussion of forecast uncertainty:

- what forecast uncertainty is,
- what it depends upon,
- how forecast uncertainty might be measured, and
- how measures of forecast uncertainty might be used in practice.

Measures of forecast uncertainty have numerous uses. For instance, prior to the realization of outcomes, a measure of forecast uncertainty provides an assessment of the expected or predicted uncertainty of the forecast errors, helping to qualify the forecasts themselves and to clarify the expected range of likely outcomes. Also, once outcomes are known, the corresponding forecast errors and the anticipated forecast uncertainty can help evaluate the models from which the forecasts were generated.

Section 5.2 examines what forecast uncertainty is, and it also considers some measures of forecast uncertainty and some possible practical consequences of forecast uncertainty. Section 5.3 discusses five possible sources of forecast uncertainty, focusing on two in particular. One is associated with future shocks to the economy, and the other arises from estimating the forecast model. Section 5.3 also highlights how anticipated forecast uncertainty is affected by the choice of variable being forecast, the type of forecast model (whether static or dynamic), the forecast horizon, the information available, and the underlying economic process. To illustrate the various issues associated with forecast uncertainty, this chapter draws on several empirical examples, including the Bank of England's inflation forecast, forecasts of the US trade balance, forecasts of the US/UK exchange rate, and forecasts of UK national income.

Some preliminary comments will aid in following the presentation below. This chapter presupposes an understanding of "how economists forecast" on the level of the presentation in Chapter 2. For the most part, the current chapter restricts itself to time-series models and econometric models as the tools for forecasting. Further, these models are assumed to be well-specified. Clements and Hendry (1998), Clements and Hendry (1999), and Ericsson and Marquez (1998) consider some of the generalizations required, and discuss the implications for situations in which the empirical forecast model is mis-specified and for which that mis-specification is important. Wallis (2000) *inter alia* discusses various ways of characterizing forecast uncertainty in macroeconomic modeling. Clements and Hendry (2001a) provide extensive summaries on myriad facets of forecasting generally. Finally, and at a very practical level, figures—which are central to this chapter's examples—often appear as panels of graphs, with each graph in a panel labeled sequentially by a suffix $a, b, c, \ldots$, left to right, row by row.

5.2   Forecasts, Outcomes, and Forecast Errors

This section discusses at an intuitive level what forecast uncertainty is, through examining forecasts, outcomes, and forecast errors. Section 5.2.1 defines and illustrates what is meant by forecast uncertainty, and Section 5.2.2 considers various measures of forecast uncertainty and some possible economic consequences of forecast uncertainty.[1]

5.2.1   Forecast uncertainty

Forecast uncertainty reflects the dispersion of possible outcomes relative to the forecast being made. Figure 5.1 illustrates this notion through the forecasts and outcomes of the US trade balance, which is the value of exports minus the value of imports. Figure 5.1a (the upper left graph in the panel) plots the forecasts from a vector autoregressive model (described in Marquez and Ericsson (1993)), along with the outcomes of the trade balance. The forecast errors are simply the outcomes minus the forecasts, and are plotted in Figure 5.1c, directly below Figure 5.1a.

These forecast errors are calculated from the observed outcomes for the trade balance. However, the outcomes could have been otherwise. The future trade balance is not known in advance, and it could take a range of values. Figure 5.1b plots an alternate sequence of outcomes for the trade balance, along with the same (original) set of forecasts; and Figure 5.1d plots the corresponding set of alternate forecast errors. Different sequences of outcomes could have occurred, implying different sequences of forecast errors. A whole range of outcomes could arise, some of them being more likely than others. That entails a distribution of forecast errors.

---

[1] Strictly speaking, "forecast uncertainty" should be called "forecast error uncertainty" because the forecast error is what is uncertain, not the forecast. However, following common usage in the literature, and for brevity's sake, the phrase "forecast uncertainty" is used throughout this chapter.

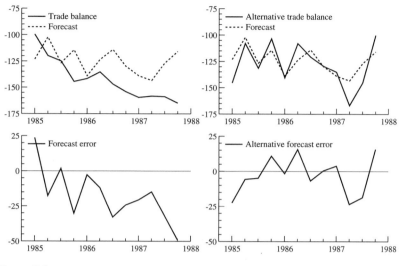

Figure 5.1
Forecasts, outcomes, and forecast errors of the US trade balance, with alternate outcomes and forecast errors of the trade balance.

Graphs provide a convenient means for expressing the distribution—and hence the uncertainty—associated with the forecast errors.   For example, the Bank of England portrays forecast uncertainty in an ingenious manner through the "fan charts" that it has been publishing recently for its forecasts of both GDP growth and inflation; see the Bank of England (2000, p. iv). Figure 5.2 reproduces the Bank's fan chart for its November 2000 forecast of RPIX inflation.[2] The Bank describes this graph as follows.

> The fan chart depicting the probability distribution for inflation is rather like a contour map. At any given point during the forecast period, the depth of shading represents the height of the probability density function over a range

---

[2]RPIX is the UK retail prices index for all items, excluding mortgage interest payments. The Bank of England's inflation target is defined in terms of RPIX inflation.

Also, note that, in the Bank of England's graph format, tick marks appear adjacent to the numbers on the right-hand side y-axis. In Figure 5.2, and in Figure 5.3 below, these numbers are always non-negative, and the tick marks should not be mis-interpreted as minus signs.

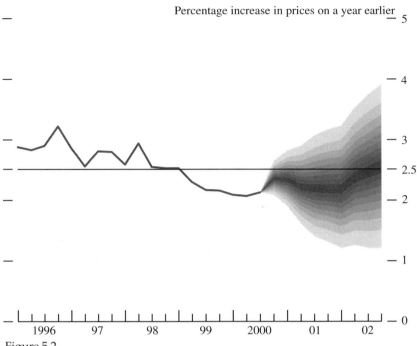

Figure 5.2
The Bank of England's November 2000 fan chart for projections of RPIX inflation.

> of outcomes for inflation. The darkest band includes the
> central (single most likely) projection and covers 10% of the
> probability. Each successive pair of bands is drawn to cover
> a further 10% of the probability, until 90% of the probability
> distribution is covered. The bands widen as the time ho-
> rizon is extended, indicating increasing uncertainty about
> outcomes. Bank of England (2000, Chart 2, p. iv)

The fan chart summarizes the Bank's predicted or anticipated probability distribution of inflation outcomes at different forecast horizons.

The Bank of England (2000, Chart 6.4, p. 66) also published the density function corresponding to that distribution at two years out—that
density appears in Figure 5.3. From Figure 5.3, the Bank's 90% confidence interval for annual inflation in the twelve months 2002Q1–2002Q4
is from 1% to 4% (approximately), as indicated by the shaded area in

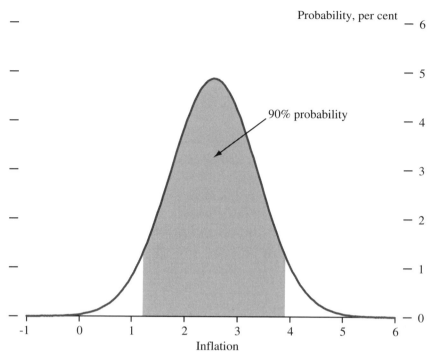

Figure 5.3
The November 2000 projection by the Bank of England for the probability density of RPIX inflation in the year to 2002Q4.

the graph. Other outcomes for inflation could occur outside that range, but the probability of those outcomes is believed to be relatively small.[3]

Until relatively recently, such portrayals of forecast uncertainty were uncommon in economics. However, in part because the Bank of England's approach to inflation targeting has become a template for a number of other central banks, the use of fan charts is also expanding. The Bank of Thailand (2000), for instance, has adopted the Bank of England's format for fan charts and probability densities in its own *Inflation*

---

[3]The density function in Figure 5.3 measures the relative frequencies of occurrence for various outcomes of inflation, as expected by the Bank of England from its inflation forecasts. The y-axis in Figure 5.3 is scaled to deliver the probability that the inflation rate is within ± 0.05 percentage points of any given value on the x-axis. For instance, from Figure 5.3, the probability of inflation being 2% per annum (i.e., between 1.95% and 2.05%) is about 4%.

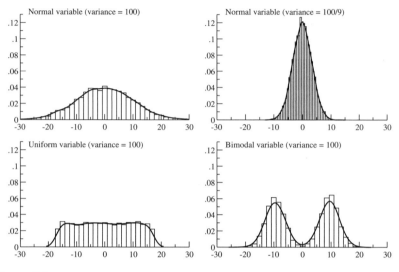

Figure 5.4

Four examples of possible histograms (displayed as rectangles) and estimated densities (—) for forecast errors.

Report. Equally important, the software for generating fan charts and the like is now readily available; see Doornik and Hendry (2001b, p. 35). See also Wallis (1999) and Chapter 8, which provide further details on fan charts and forecasting at the Bank of England.

Densities of outcomes are very useful when thinking about forecast errors, as such densities formalize which outcomes are relatively likely and which are relatively unlikely. There are many possible distributions for forecast errors, and the precise nature of those distributions can influence individuals' responses to the corresponding uncertainty. Figure 5.4 plots four possible densities with corresponding histograms to illustrate two features: the degree of dispersion, typically measured by the variance; and the generic shape of the density. The densities in Figures 5.4a and 5.4b have the same shapes—both are Gaussian, or "normal"—but the density in Figure 5.4a has a variance equal to nine times the variance for the density in Figure 5.4b. That is, the density in Figure 5.4a is much less concentrated around its mean than is the density in Figure 5.4b, implying that the range of likely outcomes in

Figure 5.4a is much wider than the corresponding range in Figure 5.4b. Thus, the forecast uncertainty in Figure 5.4a is larger than that in Figure 5.4b.

The shape of the density can vary, even for a given variance of the forecast errors. The densities in Figures 5.4a, 5.4c, and 5.4d all have the same variance: it is equal to 100, implying a standard deviation of 10. However, the densities in those figures have vastly different shapes. Figure 5.4c is a uniform distribution, with equally likely outcomes between approximately –17 and +17. Figure 5.4d illustrates a bimodal density, which here is the combination of two Gaussian densities with means of approximately –10 and +10 each.[4] The average outcome for each of the four densities in Figures 5.4a–5.4d is zero; but zero is a relatively unlikely outcome in Figure 5.4d, contrasting with (say) Figures 5.4a and 5.4b. Equally, –10 and +10 are relatively likely outcomes in Figure 5.4d, but not in Figure 5.4a, and even less so in Figure 5.4b. Bimodal densities like the one in Figure 5.4d may well characterize some economic variables, such as the depreciation rate of some exchange rates, where there might be relatively high probabilities of little depreciation and of large depreciations (e.g., as in an exchange rate crisis), but with a low probability of moderate depreciations. Bimodal densities also may arise when the mean of the variable shifts sometime in the sample being considered, as with a structural break.

5.2.2 *Measures of forecast uncertainty*

Many measures exist for summarizing properties of a forecast and its corresponding forecast error, including the bias of the forecast, the variance of the forecast error, and the mean square forecast error (MSFE), where the last combines the bias and the variance in a statistically appealing manner. In general, the whole distribution of outcomes is of interest when considering forecast uncertainty. That said, the primary

---

[4] Figure 5.4, and also Figures 5.7 and 5.8 below, plot histograms and estimated densities for several variables. A histogram is a set of vertical rectangles, with the height of each rectangle representing the variable's frequency of occurrence in the range specified by the rectangle's width. The estimated density is a smoothed interpolation of the histogram. See Doornik and Hendry (1996) for details.

In Figure 5.4, each histogram and estimated density is of 10,000 Monte Carlo (artificial) random numbers generated to have the distribution specified.

measure of forecast uncertainty in economics is the mean square forecast error, which simplifies to the variance of the forecast error when the forecast is unbiased. While Figure 5.4 highlights some shortcomings to using the variance and MSFE as measures of forecast uncertainty, the variance and MSFE still do capture important aspects of forecast uncertainty and so are considered in much of the discussion below. See Clements and Hendry (1993) for a detailed theoretical analysis of MSFEs and their limitations.

Forecast uncertainty can have many economic consequences. For instance, if the forecast uncertainty in Figure 5.4a is viewed as being considerable, insurance might be desirable as a mechanism for protecting against untoward outcomes; and different types of insurance might be available. Also, individuals may wish to take advantage of forecast uncertainty. One example is gambling, where forecast uncertainty is inherent to the activity. Likewise, investment by manufacturing firms in machinery and by individuals in the stock market are inherently risky activities, yet those activities are undertaken, with the possibility of large successes being an attraction of such investments. To summarize, forecast uncertainty is ubiquitous in economics, and many consequences may follow from the presence and extent of that uncertainty.

5.3   Sources of Forecast Uncertainty

This section examines the determinants of forecast uncertainty, focusing on two in particular: one is inherent to the uncertainty of future events, and the other depends upon the uncertainty that arises from estimating the forecast model itself. Sections 5.3.1 and 5.3.2 highlight how these two sources of predicted forecast uncertainty are affected by the type of forecast model (whether static or dynamic) and the forecast horizon. Both static and dynamic models have played important roles in forecasting; see Box and Jenkins (1970), Hendry, Pagan and Sargan (1984), Hendry (1995, Chapter 7), and Clements and Hendry (2000) *inter alia*. Section 5.3.3 briefly describes some ways in which measures of forecast uncertainty are used in economics.

Clements and Hendry (1998, Chapter 7.3, especially Table 7.1) develop a five-fold categorization for the sources of model-based forecast error:

(1) future changes in the underlying structure of the economy,
(2) mis-specification of the model,
(3) mis-measurement of the data in the base period from which fore-casting begins,
(4) inaccuracies in the estimates of the model's parameters, and
(5) the cumulation of future errors (or "shocks") to the economy.

In practice, all five sources are important when analyzing forecast un-certainty. To paraphrase Maxine Singer (1997, p. 38), the uncertainty from Items 1–3 reflects "what we don't know that we don't know". These sources of uncertainty lie beyond the scope of this chapter, but see Chapters 1, 2, and 11. By contrast, Items 4 and 5 are predictable in the sense that the degree of uncertainty arising from them can be anticipated and even calculated. These sources of uncertainty arise from "what we *do* know that we don't know". This chapter focuses on Items 4 and 5, and primarily on Item 5.

At a more prosaic level, forecast uncertainty depends upon the vari-able being forecast, the type of model used for forecasting, the eco-nomic process actually determining the variable being forecast, the in-formation available, and the forecast horizon. On the first, some vari-ables may be inherently more difficult to forecast than others. For in-stance, imports and exports each might be highly predictable, and good models might exist for forecasting them. The trade balance—that is, the value of exports minus imports—might be quite difficult to fore-cast. Specifically, by being the difference between two relatively large quantities (exports and imports), the trade balance is itself a relatively small quantity, whereas its forecast error reflects the forecast errors of both imports and exports. As another example, forecasting the level of the exchange rate might be relatively easy, in that the exchange rate in (say) a month's time is likely to be close to today's exchange rate. That said, forecasting the change in the exchange rate over the next month could be quite difficult. The particular variables being forecast and the transformations applied to those variables thus can affect the degree of forecast uncertainty present.

Secondly, forecast uncertainty depends upon the model that is being used for forecasting. Some models may simply be better for forecasting than others. Also, the precise form of the model determines the *anti-cipated* forecast uncertainty in light of that model, as distinct from the *actual* forecast uncertainty that arises. That distinction exists because a model is a simplified characterization of the economy, not a reproduction of the economy. Sometimes that characterization is a good one, and sometimes it is not.

Thirdly, and relatedly, the underlying process generating the data plays a role in determining forecast uncertainty, as by placing limits on the minimum actual forecast uncertainty obtainable from a model. That distinguishes between the predicted forecast uncertainty—that is, the forecast uncertainty that one would anticipate, given the model—and the actual forecast uncertainty, which is the uncertainty arising from the combination of the model with the actual behavior of the economic data.

Fourthly, forecast uncertainty depends upon the information available for constructing the forecasts. This aspect is closely tied to the design of the forecast model. More information would seem to be beneficial for forecasting, and it is so in some situations. However, when the model is mis-specified and there are structural breaks in the data, use of additional information can increase actual forecast uncertainty; see Clements and Hendry (1999, Chapter 2).

Finally, the forecast horizon can influence the degree of forecast uncertainty, as highlighted by the Bank of England's fan chart.

5.3.1 *Forecast uncertainty and static models*

To illustrate the notion of forecast uncertainty, this subsection considers two simple examples, one of forecasting a taxi fare, and the other of forecasting real national income for the United Kingdom. In both cases, the models are static.

Consider forecasting the taxi fare for traveling next Monday morning from my home to work. From previous cab rides, I know that the fare is calculated from the miles traveled and the time spent in the cab:

$$
\begin{aligned}
\text{fare} \;=\; & (\$2.00/\text{mile}) \times (\text{miles traveled}) \\
& + (\$0.10/\text{minute}) \times (\text{minutes in cab}). \tag{5.1}
\end{aligned}
$$

The distance traveled is 2 miles, and the time spent in the cab is 10 minutes on average. However, the actual time in the cab varies, depending upon traffic, the weather, the aggressiveness of the particular cab driver, and so on—all factors that I don't know currently. These unknown factors contribute to Item 5 above: future shocks. Thus, I might forecast a fare of $5.00. Yet, when I actually take the cab, I might have a larger or smaller fare, such as $5.30 or $4.90. The forecast uncertainty would reflect my anticipated variation in possible lengths of time spent in the cab.

Item 4 contributes to the forecast error through the imprecision in the estimates of the parameters of the model. In the taxicab example, such imprecision could arise from (e.g.) my incorrect recollection that the minute charge was $0.10/minute, rather than the actual charge of $0.20/minute, in which case the "estimated" formula above for the fare is inaccurate. Or, I could have an altogether incorrect model for the fare. The fare might actually be a flat charge between two regions of town and not depend on the time taken at all. That sort of mis-specification would fall under Item 2.

Returning to the formula above, my forecast for a typical fare might be $5.00, with a certain amount of uncertainty associated with the outcome. Unless (e.g.) some days are known to have heavier or more variable traffic than others, the forecast and the forecast uncertainty are in essence static. My forecast for next Monday's fare is the same as for next Tuesday's fare, and the anticipated distribution of forecast errors for next Monday is the same as for next Tuesday. That is, the timing of the next cab ride—in terms of the day on which it actually occurs—is unimportant for the forecast and for forecast uncertainty, other than that the ride occurs in the future.

As a second example, consider modeling real net national income in the United Kingdom over 1970–1993 and forecasting it over 1994–2010. The data are from Ericsson, Hendry and Prestwich (1998), and the model is a very simple one: namely, that real net national income (in logarithms) is equal to an intercept plus a linear trend plus an error.[5] Algebraically, the model implies the following relation for income in the first forecast period (1994):

---

[5] Even although 1994 is some years in the past, the forecast period begins in 1994 because the date of the most recent observation in Ericsson, Hendry and Prestwich's (1998) dataset is 1993.

$$\begin{aligned} \text{income}_{1994} \;=\;& \text{intercept} + (\text{coefficient} \times \text{trend}_{1994}) \\ & + \text{error}_{1994} \\ =\;& \text{intercept} + (\text{coefficient} \times 1994) \\ & + \text{error}_{1994}, \end{aligned} \tag{5.2}$$

where a subscript on a variable indicates the dating of the subscripted variable, and where the trend's coefficient captures any fixed, systematic shift in income from one period to the next. For this model, the one-year ahead forecast of income is equal to the intercept, plus the trend coefficient times the value of the trend in 1994. As the equation above indicates, the trend in 1994 equals 1994 itself. The uncertainty associated with the forecast for 1994 reflects the distribution of the error in 1994, i.e., of error_{1994}.

Consider forecasting two years ahead, rather than just one year ahead. The trend model implies that income in 1995 is:

$$\begin{aligned} \text{income}_{1995} \;=\;& \text{intercept} + (\text{coefficient} \times \text{trend}_{1995}) \\ & + \text{error}_{1995} \\ =\;& \text{intercept} + (\text{coefficient} \times 1995) \\ & + \text{error}_{1995}. \end{aligned} \tag{5.3}$$

The forecast of income in 1995 is equal to the intercept, plus the trend coefficient times the value of the trend in 1995. The uncertainty associated with this forecast reflects the distribution of the error in 1995, i.e., of error_{1995}. In general, for forecasts multiple periods ahead, the forecast error for the trend model is the model error for the period being forecast. The final period forecast (2010) is 17 periods ahead relative to the last period observed (1993), and the forecast error for 2010 is the model error for 2010, i.e., error_{2010}.

In many trend models, errors are assumed to be independent across time, and to have the same properties over time, implying that the forecast uncertainty remains constant across different forecast horizons. While the trend in (5.3) varies over time, it is deterministic, imlying that its future values are known, as well as its current and past values. Thus, this trend model is in essence static, and the anticipated forecast uncertainty is constant across different forecast horizons.

Figure 5.5a shows the results from estimating this trend model and forecasting from it. The left half of Figure 5.5a plots actual income and

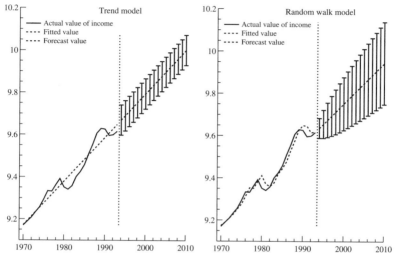

Figure 5.5
Actual, fitted, and forecast values from the trend and random-walk models of annual real net national income for the United Kingdom (in logs), with 95% confidence intervals for the forecasts.

the fitted values of income from the trend model estimated over 1970–1993. The right half of Figure 5.5a plots the model's forecasts, which date from 1994 through 2010. The vertical bars around those forecasts represent the anticipated 95% confidence intervals for income, much as the outer edges of the Bank of England's fan chart represent the Bank's anticipated 90% confidence intervals for inflation. As implied above, the 95% confidence intervals for the trend model's forecasts do not vary over the forecast horizon.

5.3.2 Forecast uncertainty and dynamic models

Drawing on examples involving UK national income, the US/UK exchange rate, and the US trade balance, this subsection shows how dynamics in a model can affect forecast uncertainty. In particular, model dynamics often imply that forecast uncertainty increases with the forecast horizon, where the latter is the length of time from the period in which the forecast is made to the period being forecast. Many economic data series are highly dynamic, in that they are characterized by strong time dependence, persistence, or memory. Visibly, the income series in Figure 5.5a has strong persistence present, as do many other economic variables, such as exchange rates, interest rates, consumers' expenditure, and inflation. Incorporation of time dependence into a forecast model often implies that forecast uncertainty increases as the forecast horizon lengthens. This feature is exemplified by the Bank of England's fan chart (Figure 5.2 above): for instance, the forecast uncertainty for 2002Q4 is larger than that for 2001Q1.

Many models imply that forecast uncertainty depends upon the forecast horizon. One model—the random-walk model—is especially useful for demonstrating that dependence, as the following example with the national income data shows. When applied to income, the random-walk model posits that income in a given period equals a constant term or intercept, plus the previous period's income, plus a shock (or error term), where the intercept captures any fixed, systematic shift in income from one period to the next. Algebraically, the model implies the following relation for income in the first period forecast (1994):

$$\text{income}_{1994} \;=\; \text{intercept} + \text{income}_{1993}$$
$$+ \text{error}_{1994}. \tag{5.4}$$

(The intercept and error in this equation generally are not the same as the intercept and error in the trend model above.) In this random-walk model, the forecast of income in 1994 is the intercept plus income in 1993, where the value of income in 1993 is known. The associated forecast uncertainty reflects the distribution of the error in the following year, i.e., of error_{1994}.

For forecasting two years ahead, the random-walk model implies:

$$\text{income}_{1995} \;=\; \text{intercept} + \text{income}_{1994} + \text{error}_{1995}$$
$$=\; (2 \times \text{intercept}) + \text{income}_{1993}$$
$$+ (\text{error}_{1994} + \text{error}_{1995}), \tag{5.5}$$

where the second equality is obtained by substitution using (5.4). The forecast of income for 1995 is the income in 1993 plus twice the value of the intercept, and the uncertainty in this forecast is owing to the distribution of the model errors in both 1994 and 1995, combined as $error_{1994} + error_{1995}$. In general, those errors don't cancel; rather, they cumulate.

For forecasts multiple periods ahead, the forecast error from the random-walk model is the sum of the model errors over the forecast horizon. So, in this model, the outcomes of future income reflect the cumulation of shocks over time, as might occur from technological innovation. For the final period forecast (2010), the corresponding forecast error is the sum of all model errors from 1994 (the first period forecast) through 2010. That is, the forecast error for 2010 is:

$$\text{forecast error}_{2010} = error_{1994} + error_{1995}$$
$$+ \cdots + error_{2009} + error_{2010}. \qquad (5.6)$$

That contrasts with the trend model's forecast error for 2010, which is just $error_{2010}$ (albeit a different "$error_{2010}$" than what appears in (5.6)).

Figure 5.5b plots the actual, fitted, and forecast values from this random-walk model of income, using the same sample periods for estimation and forecasting as with the trend model in Figure 5.5a. The confidence intervals for the random-walk forecasts in Figure 5.5b increase very substantially as the forecast horizon itself increases, contrasting with confidence intervals of fixed width in Figure 5.5a for the trend model.

Figures 5.5a and 5.5b portray two very different patterns for the anticipated forecast uncertainty, and their comparison illustrates how model choice can affect those patterns. Exactly the same time series is being modeled and forecast in Figures 5.5a and 5.5b: only the models themselves differ. More generally, static models commonly imply forecast uncertainty that is time-invariant or nearly so, whereas dynamic models typically imply time-dependent forecast uncertainty, often increasing in the forecast horizon. The trend and random-walk models above present static and dynamic relationships as black and white, but in practice a whole spectrum of models exists with both static and dynamic features.

To examine other aspects of forecast uncertainty and to highlight the consequences of dynamics in forecasting, consider another time series, that of the US/UK exchange rate. Figure 5.6a plots the level of this series, measured in $/£, over the period 1971–2000. The level of this

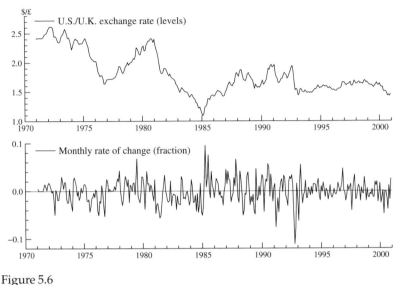

Figure 5.6
The US/UK exchange rate, and its monthly rate of change (as a fraction).

exchange rate exhibits very considerable time dependence. The value of the exchange rate in one period is very similar to its value in the previous period—hence the presence of time dependence, or persistence, or memory. Figure 5.6b plots the monthly rate of change in the exchange rate, expressed as a fraction. As is typical for many economic variables, the time dependence of the rate of change is much less than that of the original series itself.

To see the dependence of forecast uncertainty on the forecast horizon in dynamic models, consider the empirical density of the forecast error at different forecast horizons when using a random-walk model for forecasting the exchange rate. Specifically, Figure 5.7 plots the empirical densities of the forecast errors at forecast horizons of 1 month, 3 months, 6 months, 9 months, 12 months, and 24 months. As the forecast horizon increases, the density becomes flatter and the dispersion of forecast errors becomes larger, reflecting an increased dispersion of outcomes and an increased forecast uncertainty. At only two years out, the uncertainty is considerable: the majority of changes in the exchange rate are in excess of 10% in absolute value, with some changes being

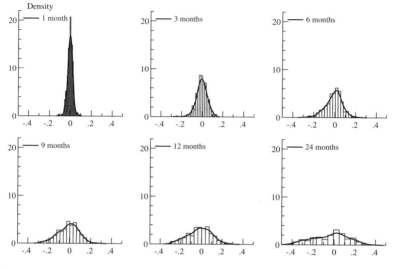

Figure 5.7
Histograms and estimated densities of forecast errors for the US/UK exchange rate at 1-, 3-, 6-, 9-, 12-, and 24-month horizons (expressed as a fraction of the exchange rate).

nearly ±50%. Empirically, the forecast uncertainty for the exchange rate depends upon the forecast horizon, with greater uncertainty at longer horizons—certainly an intuitive result.

The plots of the exchange rate and its rate of change in Figure 5.6 suggest an alteration in exchange-rate behavior after the exchange-rate crisis in 1992. From 1993 onwards, the exchange rate appears to be much more stable and to have much less volatility than previously. That characterization is also reflected in the empirical densities of the 1-month ahead forecast errors over the respective subsamples, as plotted in Figure 5.8a (for 1971–1992) and Figure 5.8b (for 1993–2000). The density of the forecast errors for the more recent period is more concentrated than the one for the period ending in 1992: that is, recent forecast errors have tended to be smaller in absolute value than ones prior to 1993. Empirically, the forecast error variance over 1993–2000 is less than half that over 1971–1992. The change in the distribution of the forecast errors suggests a change in the behavior of the exchange

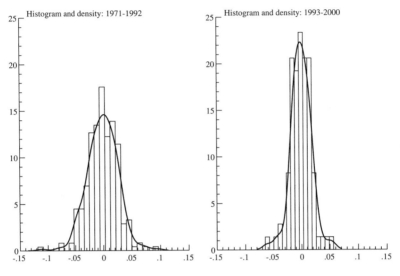

Figure 5.8

Histograms and estimated densities of one-month ahead forecast errors for the US/UK exchange rate over two subsamples: 1971–1992 and 1993–2000.

rate, which might require redesign of the forecast model. While such redesign goes beyond the scope of this chapter, it is the topic of much current research in economics; see Hendry (1987), Hendry (1995), Hoover and Perez (1999), and Krolzig and Hendry (2001) *inter alia*.

The random-walk model—examined here for both real national income and the exchange rate—embodies a very striking version of persistence, in which past shocks are felt forever into the future with their full effect. For the random-walk model, the variance of the forecast errors increases in proportion to the length of the forecast horizon. More generally, the variance of the forecast errors from a dynamic model depends both on the forecast horizon and on the degree of persistence captured by the model. Suppose that the degree of persistence is quantified by some number "p" (p for persistence), with unity ($p = 1$) characterizing the strong persistence in a random-walk model, and zero ($p = 0$) characterizing the complete lack of persistence in a static model. Degrees of persistence between zero and unity are possible, and Figure 5.9 plots how the variance of the forecast errors might depend on

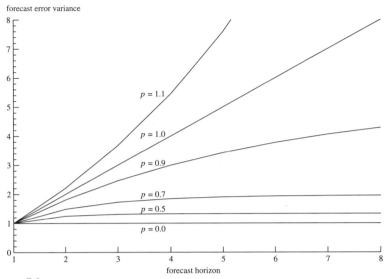

forecast error variance

Figure 5.9

Hypothetical variances of forecast errors, as a function of the degree of persistence p and of the forecast horizon (in periods).

both the degree of persistence and the forecast horizon. For models with estimated persistence less than unity, forecast uncertainty typically increases in the forecast horizon but asymptotes to some finite value, rather than increasing without bound, as it does for the random-walk model.[6]

Finally, consider a comparison across 1-period and multiple-period ahead forecasts from both static and dynamic models. Marquez and Ericsson (1993) analyze in detail the forecasts from various models of the US trade balance, and this subsection now examines forecasts from two of Marquez and Ericsson's models. The first model is essentially a static model, whereas the second model is a highly dynamic model. (In the notation of Marquez and Ericsson (1993), these are Models M1 and M5.) Figure 5.10 plots the forecasts, actual outcomes, and 95% forecast confidence intervals for each of these two models, both one quarter ahead and multiple quarters ahead. For the near-static model,

---

[6]The results in Figure 5.9 are normalized such that the one-period ahead forecast error variance is the same for all values of p and equals unity.

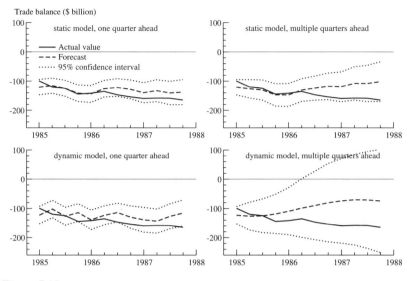

Figure 5.10

Actual (—) and forecast (– –) values from two models of the real US trade balance, both one quarter and multiple quarters ahead, with 95% confidence intervals (- - -) for the forecasts.

the width of the confidence interval varies only slightly with the forecast horizon. For the dynamic model, the width of the multi-period ahead confidence interval is highly dependent upon the forecast horizon, with much larger forecast uncertainty at longer horizons. These multi-period ahead confidence intervals are very similar in character to those in the Bank of England's fan chart. The fan shape of the confidence intervals in both instances suggests the very dynamic nature of the variable being forecast and of the implied model being used to forecast it.

5.3.3   *Measures of forecast uncertainty in practice*

Measures of forecast uncertainty have numerous uses in economic practice. Firstly, prior to the realization of outcomes, a measure of forecast uncertainty provides an assessment of expected or predicted uncertainty of the forecast errors, helping to qualify the forecasts themselves and to give a picture of the expected range of likely outcomes.

That is, information about forecast uncertainty is important in addition to the forecast itself. See Campos (1992) and Chapters 2, 7, 8, and 9 *inter alia* for empirical applications that include measures of forecast uncertainty.

Secondly, forecasts, outcomes, the corresponding forecast errors, and the anticipated forecast uncertainty can help evaluate the models from which the forecasts were generated. For instance, if the forecast errors lie well outside the range that was anticipated, that indicates specification problems with the model. Such evaluation has been central to testing and improving empirical economic models. See Chow (1960) for the initial development of these evaluation techniques; Chong and Hendry (1986), Ericsson (1992), Hansen (1992a, 1992b), Andrews (1993), and West (1996) for more recent contributions; Chapter 6 for an overview; Goldfeld (1973, 1976), Judd and Scadding (1982), and Baba, Hendry and Starr (1992) for examples in modeling the demand for money; and Marquez and Ericsson (1993) and Ericsson and Marquez (1993) for analysis of the US trade balance forecasts described above. In the future, economists could likewise examine whether the Bank of England's published confidence bands reflect what happened in the data or if those bands were too narrow or too wide. Such an analysis could benefit the construction of future monetary policy. Assessment of model forecasts is also central to evaluating the Lucas (1976) critique, with corresponding model constancy tests providing the primary empirical basis for confirming or refuting the Lucas critique; see Hendry (1988), Engle and Hendry (1993), and Ericsson and Irons (1995).

Predicted forecast uncertainty thus permits assessing how important Items 1–3 (in the forecast error taxonomy) are in contributing to the realized forecast error. Specifically, Items 1–3 reflect discrepancies between the model used for forecasting and the actual behavior of the economy, with Item 1 being primarily responsible for forecast failure in econometric models; see Chapters 2 and 11. Item 1 may arise from changes in government economic policy, as alluded to in Chapter 3's discussion of policy simulation. While the current chapter ignores Items 1–3 for expository convenience, they can be very important in practice.

Thirdly, and relatedly, the degree of forecast uncertainty present depends in fair part on the information available when forecasting. Thus, forecast uncertainty may decline if the information available for forecasting is increased and if that information affects the variables being forecast in a systematic fashion. Efforts to improve the models being used for forecasting may help reduce the implied forecast uncertainty.

Fourthly, a measure of forecast uncertainty helps distinguish between numerical accuracy and statistical accuracy in forecasts. A forecast might be numerically inaccurate, but statistically accurate. For instance, the forecast might deviate considerably numerically from actual outcomes, as in Figure 5.10d, where some of the forecast errors of the US trade balance are of the order of $80 billion, a considerable sum. Statistically, those forecast errors are well within the range anticipated from the forecast uncertainty associated with the model generating those forecasts. Conversely, forecast errors might be numerically small, but still be detectable statistically as lying outside the range of anticipated forecast uncertainty. Expressed slightly differently, a distinction exists between poor forecasts—ones that have associated numerically large forecast errors—and forecast failure, in which the forecast errors are larger than anticipated, given the forecast uncertainty associated with the forecast model.

Finally, many real-life implications follow from the degree of forecast uncertainty present. We, as individuals, make plans for the future; and what actually happens in the future affects us through those plans relative to the actual outcomes. We may thus adjust our behavior in the face of forecast uncertainty. Sometimes we may wish to protect ourselves against a range of outcomes, as by taking out insurance. For instance, we might prepay major expenses of a holiday abroad in order to avoid exchange-rate risk. Likewise, importers of goods might engage in forward contracts to protect themselves from exchange-rate risk. We may also wish to accept some uncertainty in order to take advantage of the range of potential outcomes available, as in participating in stock markets. Governments may consider the implications of forecast uncertainty and, in particular, the consequences of and costs to making forecast errors in economic policy; see Chapters 4 and 10.

5.4 Conclusions

Forecast uncertainty reflects the dispersion of possible outcomes relative to the forecast being made. Numerous measures of forecast uncertainty are available, with the variance of the forecast errors and the mean square forecast error being commonly used in practice. The entire distribution of potential outcomes may be of interest, and not just a summary measure; and graphs can aid in conveying the properties of that distribution. While this chapter has illustrated these issues with simple models, the issues themselves are generic to forecasting; see Clements and Hendry (2001a). Actual forecast models may involve both static and dynamic components, they may be mis-specified, and the forecasts themselves may be of sets of variables rather than of individual variables.

Forecast uncertainty arises both from "what we don't know that we don't know" and from "what we do know that we don't know". In econometric models, forecast uncertainty from the latter can be calculated numerically. Forecast uncertainty also depends upon the variable being forecast, the type of model used for forecasting, the economic process actually determining the variable being forecast, the information available, and the forecast horizon.

Forecast uncertainty appears intrinsic to the world in which we live, and an awareness of that uncertainty helps improve our understanding of forecasts themselves, as with the Bank of England's fan charts. Measures of forecast uncertainty also provide economists with a way of assessing the importance of unmodeled features of the economy, both directly through the calculated forecast uncertainty, and indirectly through comparison of that calculated uncertainty with the realized distribution of forecast errors.

Acknowledgments

The author is a staff economist in the Division of International Finance, Board of Governors of the Federal Reserve System, Washington, DC 20551 USA, and may be reached at ericsson@frb.gov on the Internet. The views in this chapter are solely the responsibility of the author and should not be interpreted as reflecting the views of the Board of Governors of the Federal Reserve System or of any other person associated with the Federal Reserve System. I am grateful to Julia Campos, Clive Granger, David Hendry, Jaime Marquez, John Schindler, and Hayden Smith for helpful comments and discussion; to Hayden Smith for research assistance; to Jurgen Doornik for providing me with a beta-test copy of GiveWin Version 2.00; and to the Bank of England for permission to reprint the fan chart and density function in Figures 5.2 and 5.3. All numerical results were obtained using PcGive Professional Version 9: see Doornik and Hendry (1996). Data and output listings for this chapter's empirical results are available from the author and at www.federalreserve.gov/pubs/ifdp/2001/697/default.htm on the WorldWide Web; see Ericsson (2001).

6 Evaluation of Forecasts

Clive W. J. Granger

Summary

This chapter first discusses the evaluation of economic models in general, stressing that the evaluation criterion should depend on the purpose of the model. This principle is then applied to forecast evaluation. Forecasts are made for a purpose, with those forecasts typically providing the basis for economic decisions and with the resulting forecast errors entailing economic costs. Different models generate different forecasts, and the resulting economic costs have different distributions, which can be compared across models.

6.1 Model Evaluation in Economics

Before considering the specific topic of this chapter, it is worth discussing how evaluation is handled in economics in general. The economy consists of the activities of many millions of decision makers, acting largely independently but sharing information used in forming their decisions: the economy is thus very complicated. In an attempt to capture the main features of the economy, economists typically use models, either theoretical in form or empirical. The theoretical models are constructed from logic, mathematics, and sets of generally agreed-upon behavior by economic agents in the form of axioms and assumptions. The empirical models arise from the analysis of economic data, possibly at least partially based on economic theory.

In practice there are many different ways to build a model, which is good: one gets alternative models. Among the many questions that then arise, two are central to this chapter.

a. Is a given model any good? For instance, does it represent the main features of some segment of the actual economy that is of interest?
b. Which of two (or more) models is better?

These are not just academic questions but have practical implications. Question (b) is actually easier to answer than question (a): for (b), one only needs to agree on a criterion and apply it.

The field of economics naturally involves many evaluations. For example, consumers evaluate alternative goods by considering utility values, a private investor evaluates assets (such as stocks) in terms of expected returns and risks, and a company or corporation evaluates alternative capital investments using estimated flows of future returns. In the last two examples, forecasts are involved.

To evaluate an economic model, it is essential to know its purpose. Was it built to provide forecasts, to help with a policy decision, or test a specific economic hypothesis? Without having a stated or known purpose, one may accidentally apply an inappropriate criterion and thus draw a wrong conclusion. As an analogy, one might ask a member of a primitive tribe to evaluate a fork. That individual may try to hammer a nail with it and find that it is ineffective, not realizing that the fork is designed for eating purposes. Many academic papers introduce models without a specific purpose, instead saying something vague, such as that the models will "help to understand" or "learn" about some topic. The trouble here is that it is difficult to know if these objectives have been achieved. You only know if you understand something if you can prove that you can use the model, or tool, for some relevant purpose. A teenager from a Western culture may claim that he or she understands how to eat with chopsticks, but the real test is in actually doing so.

With this in mind, Section 6.2 provides a brief background on forecasting. Section 6.3 then considers the evaluation of a specific common case: the point forecast. Sections 6.4 and 6.5 discuss the evaluation of forecasts in different situations and the dependence of decisions on forecasts respectively. Section 6.6 offers a few concluding remarks.

6.2 Forecasting Background

As background for discussing the evaluation of forecasts, this section establishes a framework for describing forecasts and the discrepancies between forecasts and outcomes.

Suppose that we have a variable of interest, measured each month, denoted by X_t: an example might be the local unemployment rate. The values taken by this variable over some past period are recorded. They are called the sample $\{X_1, X_2, \ldots, X_{n-1}, X_n\}$, where n denotes "now". At time n, we look ahead h periods to X_{n+h}, the value taken by the variable X at time $n + h$. If "now" is February, we may be interested in the unemployment rate in May, which is X_{n+3}: the horizon here is $h = 3$ (i.e., 3 months hence). Because this unemployment rate has not yet happened, and because it will be influenced by many unexpected events, or stochastic shocks, it is appropriate to consider X_{n+3} as a random variable.

As a random variable, X_{n+h} can be characterized by a distribution function, denoted $F_{n,h}(x)$:

$$F_{n,h}(x) = \text{prob}(X_{n+h} \leq x), \tag{6.1}$$

where $\text{prob}(X_{n+h} \leq x)$ denotes the probability of X_{n+h} being no greater than the value x. In practice, we use a set of information available at time n to construct this distribution function, thus obtaining a *conditional* distribution function, denoted $F_{n,h}(x \mid \mathcal{I}_n)$:

$$F_{n,h}(x \mid \mathcal{I}_n) = \text{prob}([X_{n+h} \leq x] \mid \mathcal{I}_n), \tag{6.2}$$

where $\mathcal{I}_n$ represents the information available at time n, and the symbol $\mid$ denotes conditioning. The corresponding predictive probability *density* function is denoted $p_{n,h}(x \mid \mathcal{I}_n)$, where:

$$p_{n,h}(x \mid \mathcal{I}_n)\, dx = \text{prob}([x < X_{n+h} \leq x + dx] \mid \mathcal{I}_n). \tag{6.3}$$

The choice of the information included in $\mathcal{I}_n$ is extremely important when calculating the conditional distribution function. For forecasting, the information $\mathcal{I}_n$ usually consists of the present and past of a group of plausible variables. When forecasting unemployment, for example, $\mathcal{I}_n$ might include figures for production, investment, and inflation. The information $\mathcal{I}_n$ also typically includes X_{n-j} for $j > 0$, i.e., the lags on the series being forecast. The information $\mathcal{I}_n$ can include forecasts or expectations of variables, but not actual future values.

Rather than providing a variable's full predictive distribution when forecasting, confidence intervals are sometimes given instead. A confidence interval is a pair of numbers—denoted $\underline{A}_{n,h}$ and $\overline{A}_{n,h}$—for which:

$$\text{prob}\left([X_{n+h} < \underline{A}_{n,h}] \mid \mathcal{I}_n\right) = \frac{p}{2} \tag{6.4}$$

and

$$\text{prob}\left([X_{n+h} > \overline{A}_{n,h}] \mid \mathcal{I}_n\right) = \frac{p}{2} \tag{6.5}$$

for some specified level p. If p is 0.05 (say), then the interval $[\underline{A}_{n,h}, \overline{A}_{n,h}]$ is the 95% confidence interval. Thus, a forecaster might predict that the unemployment rate in three months' time will lie between 6.2% to 7.4% with a probability of 95%, in which case [6.2%, 7.4%] is the 95% confidence interval.

That said, the typical forecast is given as just a single number, denoted $f_{n,h}$ (say), which in some sense represents the middle of the whole predictive distribution. An example of such a point forecast is that "the unemployment rate in three months' time will be 6.9%". This number might represent a best guess in some sense, but it fails to indicate the uncertainty associated with it. This uncertainty is partially captured by the confidence interval and is completely described by the predictive conditional distribution. Summary statistics for the predictive conditional distribution abound. Those often reported are the conditional mean $\mu_{n,h}$ and the conditional variance $\sigma^2_{n,h}$, both of which can be derived directly from the predictive conditional distribution.

At each "now", any specific empirical model may produce forecasts, confidence intervals, and conditional variances across different horizons h. For "now" at time n, these values are denoted:

$$f_{n,1}, f_{n,2}, \ldots, f_{n,h};$$
$$[\underline{A}_{n,1}, \overline{A}_{n,1}], [\underline{A}_{n,2}, \overline{A}_{n,2}], \ldots, [\underline{A}_{n,h}, \overline{A}_{n,h}]; \text{ and}$$
$$\sigma^2_{n,1}, \sigma^2_{n,2}, \ldots, \sigma^2_{n,h}. \tag{6.6}$$

The model then produces new sets of values as "now" moves forward: that is, as n goes to $n+1$, then to $n+2$, and so forth.

We wish to evaluate these forecasts, and for several reasons. Evaluation helps us learn from previous mistakes. It also allows us to compare alternative forecasting methods and so to concentrate on those methods that are more successful. Evaluation is important for any economic model, and particularly for financial and forecasting models.

6.3 Evaluation of a Point Forecast

This section thus turns to the evaluation of forecasts. To illustrate, consider evaluating the simple one-step ahead point forecast.

Let f_n be the (one-step ahead) point forecast of X_{n+1}, where f_n is made at time n. The corresponding forecast error e_n is:

$$e_n = X_{n+1} - f_n. \tag{6.7}$$

The forecast error is not known until time $n + 1$, when X_{n+1} occurs. In economics, one can be assured from experience that there will be error.

The user of the forecast, who we will also call the decision maker, is not usually the producer of the model that gives the forecasts. Suppose that the decision maker has a cost associated with the size of the error: call that relation a cost function and denote it by $C(\cdot)$. If there is no error, one should expect a zero cost:

$$C(0) = 0. \tag{6.8}$$

Typically, the cost of a given error e increases as e itself increases in magnitude. A commonly used cost function is the squared function:

$$C(e) = e^2, \tag{6.9}$$

which is symmetric in e and which has many mathematical advantages. In practice, however, one would not typically expect the cost function to be symmetric, as three examples highlight.

- The cost of being ten minutes early for an airplane departure is quite different from the cost of being ten minutes late.
- If a lecturer does not know how many students will be in a class, the cost of requesting too big a lecture room is not the same as the cost of requesting too small a room.

- If a business person has to buy a new computer, the cost of getting one with too much memory is different from the cost of getting one with too little memory.

Formally, these asymmetries in the cost function can be expressed mathematically as $C(e) \neq C(-e)$ for some nonzero forecast error e.

Once a user of forecasts develops his or her cost function and the producer (or forecaster) provides a predictive distribution function, the point forecast is chosen as the value that minimizes the expected cost with that predictive distribution. Formally, the point forecast solves the following problem:

$$\min_{f_n} \int_{-\infty}^{\infty} C\left(f_n - x\right) p_n\left(x\right) dx, \tag{6.10}$$

where $C(\cdot)$ is the cost function described above, and $p_n\left(x\right)$ is a simplified notation for the conditional probability density function $p_{n,1}\left(x \mid \mathcal{I}_n\right)$, which is generated at time n for a forecast horizon $h = 1$. For some cost functions, the optimum point forecast f_n is just a function of the conditional mean and conditional variance of $p_n\left(x\right)$, i.e., of μ_n and σ_n^2. For example, if $C(e) = e^2$, then $f_n = \mu_n$: the optimal point forecast is just the conditional mean.

For most realistic, asymmetric cost functions, however, one has to find f_n by directly minimizing the integral in (6.10). That said, most econometric models provided only μ_n as a forecast. A few do give σ_n^2 or a confidence interval $[\underline{A}_n, \overline{A}_n]$ as well, and a very few provide estimates of $p_n\left(x\right)$. Still, interest in this area is increasing, particularly as data become more plentiful and computing becomes more inexpensive.

Although the formula (6.10) is often not easy to use, some properties can be derived for the forecasts and associated forecast errors that solve the minimization problem in (6.10). Let C' ($= dC(e)/de$) be the derivative of C with respect to e; and denote $C'(e_n)$ as W_n, where here e_n is the forecast error resulting from the minimization in (6.10). The series W_n can be shown to have what are known as "white-noise properties". First, the expectation (i.e., the mean) of W_n is zero: $\mathsf{E}(W_n) = 0$. Second, the correlation between W_n and any past W_n is also zero: $\mathrm{corr}(W_n, W_{n-j}) = 0$ for all $j > 0$. Because the cost function $C(\cdot)$ is known, these properties can be used to check whether the actual forecast has some of the properties of the optimal forecast.

6.4 Different Situations for Evaluation

When evaluating forecasts, different situations may arise, depending upon the numbers of producers and consumers of forecasts, the forecast information provided by the producers, and the cost functions of the consumers. The following assumptions help in describing some of those situations.

- *There are several producers of forecasts.* Producers of forecasts either all provide full conditional distributions, or they provide point forecasts based on their own cost functions. Producers do not necessarily have the cost functions of users, i.e., of the consumers of the forecasts. There certainly is no reason to believe that a producer's cost function should be the same as that of any consumer.
- *There are several consumers of forecasts.* Each consumer of forecasts has his or her own cost function.

This section considers some implications of these assumptions.

If each forecaster provides a predictive distribution, a consumer can use his or her cost function to produce point forecasts and, if desired, to calculate average costs based on each predictive distribution. The consumer can then choose the producer with the smallest (anticipated) average cost—smallest for that consumer's particular cost function. Each consumer may undertake this exercise. Consumers may reach different conclusions as to which producer of forecasts is best, as they (the consumers) may differ in their cost functions.

If each producer gives only a point forecast f_n, a consumer still can calculate the corresponding forecast error e_n $(= X_{n+1} - f_n)$. Over time, that consumer can construct the (sample) average cost associated with that producer, i.e.:

$$\frac{1}{N} \sum_{j=0}^{N-1} C(e_{n+j}), \tag{6.11}$$

where the producer (over time) generates N one-step ahead forecasts, resulting in the sequence of forecast errors $\{e_n, e_{n+1}, \ldots, e_{n-(N-2)}, e_{n+(N-1)}\}$. The consumer can then compare this average cost across producers to determine which producer generated point forecasts with the lowest average cost. Again, different users may prefer forecasts from different producers, as they (the users) may have different cost functions.

Could every consumer prefer one forecaster over all others, irrespective of the cost function being applied? In principle, yes. For simplicity, consider just two producers with sequences of one-step ahead point forecasts $\{f_n^{(1)}\}$ and $\{f_n^{(2)}\}$ respectively, resulting in sequences of forecast errors $\{e_n^{(1)}\}$ and $\{e_n^{(2)}\}$. Suppose that these errors are drawn from distributions $Q^{(1)}(x)$ and $Q^{(2)}(x)$, and that these distributions do not change over time. The question being asked is whether every consumer would prefer $f_n^{(1)}$ (say) over $f_n^{(2)}$, for whatever cost function he or she might have. In fact, all consumers will prefer the first producer of forecasts over the second if the distribution function $Q^{(1)}(x)$ has a property known as "convex-loss stochastic dominance". While this property is too technical to examine here, a brief description appears in my recent book, Granger (1999).

6.5 Forecasts and Decisions

The discussion so far has not linked the forecasts being made to the decisions based on the forecasts. Forecasts should be evaluated in terms of the success of the corresponding decisions. This section shows how that can be done.

The sequence of events can be considered as follows.

- Time n.

  The producer generates $p_n\,(X_{t+1}\mid \mathcal{I}_n)$, which is the predictive distribution of X_{n+1} based on some information set $\mathcal{I}_n$.

  In light of the predictive distribution $p_n\,(X_{t+1}\mid \mathcal{I}_n)$ and (possibly) other information Z_n, the user (i.e., the decision maker) then takes a decision $d_n(p_n, Z_n)$ at time n.

- Time $n+1$.

  The variable of interest X_{n+1} is now observed, and its consequences are felt. The achieved value (or utility) of the decision $d_n(p_n, Z_n)$ depends both on the event X_{n+1} and on the decision $d_n(p_n, Z_n)$ previously made. We denote that value as $V_{n+1}(X_{n+1}, d_n)$. The consequences of the decision may be expensive, and the quality of the forecast will in general influence the value $V_{n+1}(X_{n+1}, d_n)$.

Table 6.1

Values V arising from different events and decisions, and forecast and subjective probabilities for the events.

Event	Decision		Forecast	Subjective
	Yes (Y)	No (N)	probability	probability
Good (G)	V_{GY}	V_{GN}	$P_{G,n}$	$q_{G,n}$
Bad (B)	V_{BY}	V_{BN}	$P_{B,n}$	$q_{B,n}$

Granger and Pesaran (2000a) illustrate this situation with the following simple example. Suppose that some event will occur at time $n + 1$ and that it can be classified as either good (G) or bad (B). The producer of forecasts assigns *ex ante* probabilities $P_{G,n}$ and $P_{B,n}$ to those outcomes occurring, where:

$$P_{G,n} = F_{n,1} \left([X_{n+1} = G] \mid \mathcal{I}_n \right)$$

and

$$P_{B,n} = F_{n,1} \left([X_{n+1} = B] \mid \mathcal{I}_n \right)$$

in a notation like that in equation (6.2). The subscript n emphasizes that the probabilities $P_{G,n}$ and $P_{B,n}$ are generated at time n, prior to the good or bad event occurring. Also, the forecaster assumes that no other outcomes are possible, so $P_{G,n} + P_{B,n} = 1$. Before the event occurs, the decision maker must decide either to take some action (denoted Y for "yes") or not to take that action (denoted N for "no"). Four cases result from the pairings of possible events and decisions: GY, GN, BY, and BN. In each case, a particular value V arises, as detailed in Table 6.1. For instance, V_{GY} is the value coming to the decision maker if the good event occurs and a "yes" decision was taken, i.e., $V_{GY} = V_{n+1}(G_{n+1}, Y_n)$. The values V_{GN}, V_{BY}, and V_{BN} are similarly defined. Some or all of these values can be negative.

As a policy example, consider a central bank that is concerned about inflation outcomes. For this central bank, inflation being less than $2\frac{1}{2}\%$ is a good event, whereas inflation being $2\frac{1}{2}\%$ or more is a bad event. As a policy decision maker, this central bank takes action of some kind if the forecast probability of a bad event is at least 0.6 (say), and it does not take action if that probability is less than 0.6. See Chapters 4, 8, and 10 for detailed discussions on the actual role of forecasts in central bank policy decisions and on the costs resulting from the corresponding forecast errors.

Another example provides an even more concrete illustration. Consider a city government asking: "What will happen if local roads ice up tonight?" Icy roads are the bad event. Putting sand and grit on the roads is a "yes" decision, whereas not doing so is a "no" decision; and a decision must be taken before it is known whether icy conditions will occur. The four possible values for V depend on the cost of treating the roads, on whether or not the roads are treated, and on whether or not the roads are in fact icy. One would expect the following inequalities:

$$V_{BY} > V_{BN}, \qquad V_{BN} < V_{GN}, \qquad V_{GN} > V_{GY}. \tag{6.12}$$

The last inequality reflects that sanding is expensive, and that sanding is not required when the roads are not icy.

All this said, two separate issues remain—how to *make* decisions, and how to *evaluate* decisions. The area of study known as decision theory is mostly concerned with the first of these. In a decision-theoretic framework, the decision maker assigns some subjective (personal) probabilities $q_{G,n}$ and $q_{B,n}$ to the good and bad events occurring at time $n+1$. Then the decision maker forms the expected value (sometimes called the "utility") of the "yes" decision DY_n:

$$\mathsf{E}\left[DY_n\right] = q_{G,n}V_{GY} + q_{B,n}V_{BY}, \tag{6.13}$$

and similarly of the "no" decision DN_n:

$$\mathsf{E}\left[DN_n\right] = q_{G,n}V_{GN} + q_{B,n}V_{BN}. \tag{6.14}$$

(As with the forecast probabilities, we assume that the subjective probabilities add up to unity, i.e., that $q_{G,n} + q_{B,n} = 1$.) At time n, the decision maker would prefer the "yes" decision if:

$$\mathsf{E}\left[DY_n\right] > \mathsf{E}\left[DN_n\right], \tag{6.15}$$

and the "no" decision if:

$$\mathsf{E}\left[DY_n\right] < \mathsf{E}\left[DN_n\right]. \tag{6.16}$$

The subjective probabilities could just be forecasts taken from some professional forecaster, or from an appropriate model, corrected for any systematic bias.

To *evaluate* such a decision, suppose that V_{n+1} $(= V_{n+1}(X_{n+1}, d_n))$ is now an economic measure of the costs associated with the observed outcome X_{n+1} and the decision d_n made at time n. Observing a sequence of these decisions will result in a sequence of values, and an average value can be formed. Similarly, one can work out what values would have been achieved from a different set of decisions based on another forecasting model, from which another average value can be estimated. These two methods for forecasting the probabilities can then be compared by looking at the relative sizes of the economic values associated with using the decisions based on the alternative forecasts.

Granger and Pesaran (2000b) give the following application of this procedure. Consider an investment portfolio that contains either government bonds or an index of the complete stock market, with monthly switching between the two based on a forecast of the direction of change of the two possible portfolios. The value V is the average return on the portfolio, after allowing for transaction costs. Granger and Pesaran (2000b) found that forecasts based on inflation proved superior to those not using inflation, in that the resulting decisions produced similar average returns at lower risk levels.

6.6 Concluding Remarks

In evaluating economic models, the evaluation criterion should depend on the purpose of the model. This principle applies in particular to forecast evaluation: forecasts are made for a purpose. Forecasts typically provide the basis for economic decisions, and the resulting forecast errors entail economic costs. Different models generate different forecasts, and the resulting economic costs have different distributions, which can be compared across models. It is hoped that eventually all forecasts will be evaluated in this way, although doing so in practice is not always very easy.

7 Forecasting and the UK Business Cycle

Denise R. Osborn, Marianne Sensier, and Paul W. Simpson

Summary

This chapter examines the forecasting of economic activity over the business cycle. Because recessions are relatively rare events, only a few observations on them are available, and that makes modeling and forecasting recessions particularly difficult. The chapter examines a class of regime-switching models that include a short-term interest rate as a leading indicator to provide predictive information about future regimes. Large increases in the interest rate raise the probability of switching out of an expansion into a recession a year later, whereas, in a recession, even small decreases in the interest rate help start a recovery. The analysis highlights the importance of the interest-rate decisions taken by the Monetary Policy Committee at the Bank of England, and the need for the Monetary Policy Committee to look well ahead when making interest-rate decisions.

7.1 Introduction

Since the 1970s, recessions have re-emerged in the United Kingdom and other developed countries as an occasional feature within a pattern of overall economic growth. Sometimes, economic forecasters have been criticized because (at least to date) they have been largely unable to forecast either the onset of a recession or the beginning of the subsequent recovery. This inability was highlighted by the most recent UK recession, which occurred during the early 1990s. Allsopp, Jenkinson and Morris (1991) place part of the blame for this recession on forecast errors—they see the recession's roots in the boom of the late 1980s and the failure of forecasters to predict the concurrent rapid increase in consumer spending. Having failed to appreciate the extent of the boom, forecasters then did not foresee the recession, even when it was imminent. Subsequently, once the economy clearly had entered a recession, forecasters incorrectly predicted that it would recover in the near future.

With the benefit of hindsight, the UK forecasts published each quarter by the independent and respected National Institute of Economic and Social Research in their *National Institute Economic Review* provide fascinating reading over this period. As late as August 1990, no decline in real gross domestic product was foreseen. By November 1990, a decline was estimated to occur through the second half of 1990, to be followed by a steady recovery. Throughout 1991 and 1992, the National Institute continued to forecast an imminent recovery from the recession. See Chapters 4, 9, and 10 for additional analysis of this period.

At least two central questions arise when criticizing economic forecasters for missing such turning points.

- Can the forecasting tools used by economists recognize the features that distinguish recessions from expansions?
- Is sufficient information available to enable the economist to capture these distinctive features within a model and then to use this model successfully in forecasting?

In addressing these questions, we focus on the UK recession in the early 1990s.

As the previous paragraphs imply, the "business cycle" is understood to consist of two types of periods—recessions and expansions. Although not a formal definition, a recession is widely regarded as a period of prolonged decline in output experienced across much of the economy. To be more concrete, commentators often consider a recession to be in progress when total output (real gross domestic product) has declined for at least two consecutive quarters. Thus, recessions are more extensive than a single quarter's fall in output. A single period of decline may occur within an overall business-cycle expansion, as may a single period of positive growth within a recession. By distinguishing between recessions and expansions, economists and commentators alike are attempting to identify shifts in the economy's direction that are more fundamental than simple short-lived blips.

Unfortunately, even from a historical perspective, there is no widely accepted dating of expansions and recessions for the United Kingdom. For the United States, the historical classification by the National Bureau of Economic Research (NBER) is generally accepted as the authoritative dating of the US's business cycles. As Birchenhall, Jessen, Osborn and Simpson (1999) note, the NBER classification implies that the US economy has been in recessions for approximately 15% of the postwar period. Dow (1998) *inter alia* identifies three recessions in the United Kingdom postwar: the mid-1970s, the early 1980s, and the early 1990s. Those recessions imply a percentage of time spent in recessions during the postwar period that is similar to that for the United States. Section 7.2 contains more information on UK recession dates.

Notably, recessions are relatively rare events. With only three UK recessions in more than forty years, it may be difficult to extract the signals that predict the beginning of a recession. This problem would exist, even if each of these recessions contained the same identifiable characteristics that indicated, in advance, that it would (or was likely to) occur. Dow (1998) attributes the first two of these recessions at least partly to external events (particularly the increases in oil prices due to OPEC), whereas he views the third as having its origins purely in domestic factors. These differences imply additional difficulties in forecasting these recessions. Nevertheless, during these major periods of decline, the models used by economists might at least recognize that the economy is in a recession.

Because recessions are rare events, then so also are the beginnings of recoveries. We still might be more optimistic about economic models for forecasting a recovery than about those for forecasting the onset of a recession. After all, if the economy is in a recession, a major objective of macroeconomic policy will be to facilitate the beginning of a recovery.

Given that recessions and expansions have distinctive characteristics, it is natural to ask if the relationships between economic variables also differ across these two business-cycle phases. A large academic literature discusses this topic, which is often labeled "business-cycle asymmetries". Research on asymmetry typically focuses on only a single variable in isolation. The variable in question is often a labor market measure, such as unemployment, as in Acemoglu and Scott (1994) for the United Kingdom. A deeper question concerns whether economic policy has distinct effects over the business cycle. A formal examination is fraught with difficulty, again because relatively few observations on recessions are available for any one country over the postwar period. We thus are modest in our empirical analysis of recessions, focusing on how changes in interest rates affect UK output growth. We consider models that allow interest rates to affect output differentially in recessions and expansions. In particular, interest rates may differentially influence the probabilities that the economy will move from an expansion to a recession and from a recession to an expansion.

Interest rates are the key monetary tool of UK macroeconomic policy. Interest rates are now set by the Bank of England's Monetary Policy Committee, which has the primary goal of meeting the Government's inflation target: see Chapter 8. Allsopp *et al.* (1991) and Dow (1998) also see interest rates as important in having triggered the 1990s recession. Thus, our discussion aims to illuminate a highly topical issue: the effects of the Bank of England's interest-rate decisions on the real economy.

Section 7.2 outlines the nature of the postwar UK business cycle in terms of recessions and expansions. Sections 7.3 and 7.4 discuss the modeling of output growth as a univariate variable and as a function of interest-rate changes respectively. In both cases, regime-switching models are used, where these models allow for different dependencies in expansions and recessions. These models are contrasted with linear models, which economists have commonly used when forecasting. Section 7.5 numerically compares the forecasts from the linear and regime-switching models over the 1990s. Finally, Section 7.6 draws some conclusions. This chapter focuses on business-cycle forecasting throughout, and the scarcity of observations on recessions is a recurring theme.

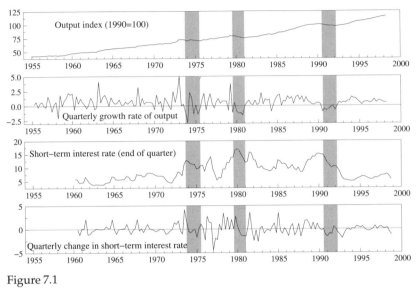

Figure 7.1

Output and interest rates over the UK business cycle.

7.2　The Nature of the UK Business Cycle

This section examines graphically the business cycles in postwar Britain. As already explained, the business cycle is partitioned into two distinct phases or regimes, which are expansions and recessions in total output. Real gross domestic product (GDP) is the generally accepted measure of overall output for the economy, and real GDP is used to measure output throughout this chapter.

Figure 7.1 illustrates what is meant by the UK business cycle in two ways: through the level of quarterly GDP (Figure 7.1a), and through its percentage quarterly growth rate (Figure 7.1b).[1] As with almost all business-cycle analyses, these series are seasonally adjusted. The data extend over 1955Q1–1998Q1; see Simpson, Osborn and Sensier (2001) for a more detailed analysis.

In Figure 7.1a, the three major postwar recessions are visible as declines in UK output. From its peak in 1973Q3 to its trough in 1975Q3,

---

[1] To be precise, the growth rate used here is computed as 100 times the difference between the (natural) logarithm of GDP at period t and its logarithim at period $t-1$.

GDP declined by 3.5%. Although the precise dates of this recession are not clear-cut, a simple mechanical rule applied to GDP growth by Birchenhall, Osborn and Sensier (2001) classifies the eight quarters following the 1973 peak as a single recession.[2] In Figure 7.1b, this recession appears as a cluster of negative values during 1973–1975. That said, three of the eight quarters within this recession exhibit positive output growth.

The dates of the two subsequent recessions are generally clearer than those of the first. It is reasonable to date 1979Q2 as ending the expansion of the late 1970s. Although output fell in 1979Q3 and then rose in 1979Q4, the increase in 1979Q4 is an isolated occurrence, as several declines immediately follow. Furthermore, GDP in 1979Q2 was higher than in 1979Q4. This recession extended until 1981Q1 and covered seven quarters, during which output fell 5.4%. The recession of the 1990s, covering the eight quarters 1990Q3–1992Q2 and representing a total decline of 3.7%, is particularly clear-cut. The mechanical rules of Birchenhall *et al.* (2001) obtain the same dates, confirming this visual dating from Figure 7.1.

A few points are worth noting. First, to aid interpretation, the three UK recessions just discussed are shaded in Figure 7.1. Second, the rule of thumb using "two quarterly declines" indicates a recession around the end of 1962, but, because the total decline is relatively small (0.8%), this episode is not considered to be a recession. Third, from Figure 7.1b, the 1990s recession differs from the other two recessions in that it does not contain any single quarter in which output falls by more than 1%. Both previous recessions include a number of quarterly declines exceeding 1%. Finally, the most recent expansion is unusually smooth by historical standards.

Figure 7.1 also graphs the interest rate used later. It is a short-term interest rate—the yield on three-month UK Treasury Bills as quoted at the end of each quarter. This series is available from 1960Q2. Figure 7.1c plots the interest rate itself, while Figure 7.1d plots its change, i.e., the interest rate's value in one quarter minus its value in the previous

---

[2]The principal difficulty in dating this recession is in deciding whether this period covers one recession or two. GDP declined in both 1973Q4 and 1974Q1, increased for each of the next two quarters, and then declined again. While GDP took its overall minimum value in 1974Q1 rather than 1975Q3, we take the latter as dating the trough of this single recession.

quarter.[3] Again, shaded areas demarcate the recessions as dated above. Interest rates are high at the beginning of each recession and then generally decline as the recession progresses. This decline is hardly surprising: monetary policy is liable to be relaxed during recessions so as to facilitate a recovery. Nevertheless, the effect of the interest rate on output is not transparent from Figure 7.1, so we delay further discussion until Section 7.4.

7.3 Univariate Business-cycle Models

Expansions and recessions clearly exhibit different properties. Although the duration and extent of decline are important, the key characteristic of a recession is the fall in economic activity. A statistical model designed to capture expansions and recessions thus will need to allow for different mean growth rates in output across these two phases. In business-cycle models, these phases are often referred to as regimes. During a recessionary regime, mean growth is negative; in an expansion regime, mean growth is positive. To be useful in forecasting, a model also needs some mechanism to predict the switch from an expansion to a recession and *vice versa*.

Before considering *nonlinear* models for capturing the characteristics of the business cycle as just outlined, this section examines the standard *linear* model, which serves as a useful benchmark. Economists conventionally use linear statistical models for forecasting and general empirical modeling. These models imply that all characteristics of the variable under analysis are constant over time, at least conditional on any right-hand side "exogenous" variables. Consequently, in these linear models, the underlying properties of the variable analyzed do not differ between recessions and expansions, except insofar as the exogenous variables differ across phases of the business cycle.

For the United Kingdom, positive output growth dominates the postwar period. In a linear univariate framework (which has no exogenous variables), the output growth in Figure 7.1b leads to a very simple specification: output growth for any future quarter is forecast

---

[3]Simpson *et al.* (2001) investigate a number of interest-rate measures when modeling output growth. Using model-selection criteria, the Treasury Bill yield is selected over competing interest rates in both linear and nonlinear model specifications.

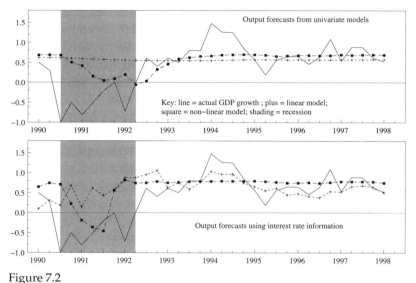

Figure 7.2

Output forecasts from univariate models and from models using interest-rate information.

to be $+0.58\%$ with a forecast standard deviation of 1%. In modeling output growth in a linear framework, past output growth is statistically insignificant, so current output growth has no role in forecasting future growth. Mills (1995) and Simpson *et al.* (2001) *inter alia* have used this type of model to describe UK output growth; see also Chapters 2, 3, and 5.

Figure 7.2a shows the forecasts from 1990Q1 onwards as produced by this univariate linear model, together with actual quarterly GDP growth. The linear forecasts form a virtually straight horizontal line because each forecast for the next quarter is approximately 0.58% growth.[4] As before, shading indicates the 1990s recession. This model attributes the difference between each outcome and the corresponding forecast to a random shock. Hence, the recession is "explained" only

---

[4]The forecasts in Figure 7.2a are one-step ahead forecasts, whereby the model is estimated up through some quarter t, with this estimated model producing the forecast for the period immediately following, which is at $t + 1$. This re-estimation has little effect on the forecasts because the mean growth rate is relatively unaffected by adding observations from 1990 onwards.

in that it derives from a chance sequence of predominantly negative shocks to output. Because future shocks are (by definition) unforecastable, the univariate linear model is unable to forecast the onset of a recession.

This linear univariate model cannot recognize that the economy is in a recession. The model is dominated by the many quarters of positive growth in the postwar economy: irrespective of the recent past, the model always forecasts positive growth for the next quarter. Even although the forecasting models used in practice are rarely univariate, forecasts from actual forecasting models have sometimes shared this characteristic with univariate models. For instance, through much of the 1990s recession, many well-respected UK forecasters continued to forecast a recovery in the near future. The very simple univariate model captures something of that forecasting problem confronting practitioners. Inclusion of lagged growth rates might help the linear model track recessions better, but (as already noted) lagged output growth does not have any substantial explanatory role, statistically speaking.

This section began by describing how nonlinear models and, more specifically, regime-switching models might help forecast the business cycle. While several types of regime-switching models have appeared in the recent literature, the Markov regime-switching model adopted by Hamilton (1989) is particularly attractive. First, it allows mean growth rates to differ across regimes. As discussed, that characteristic is necessary to capture the distinctive features of expansions and recessions. Second, the probabilistic framework of the Markov regime-switching model can embody in a natural way the idea that a specific recession or expansion regime will persist for a number of quarters. Timo Teräsvirta and some of his co-authors adopt an alternative regime-switching framework; see Teräsvirta and Anderson (1992) and Granger and Teräsvirta (1993) *inter alia*. Their approach allows mean growth rates to differ across regimes, but it does not directly incorporate regime persistence. We consider this latter feature to be important in modeling and forecasting business cycles, so we focus on Markov regime-switching models.

It is not our intention to go into technical modeling details. Hamilton (1989) includes these, as do many subsequent studies that have extended the methodology and applied it broadly. Nevertheless, we do outline the principles underlying the model. See Simpson *et al.* (2001) for a full description of the approach taken and of the detailed UK results on which we draw. While applications of the Markov regime-switching model typically analyze US data, as in Filardo (1994), Diebold and Chen (1996), and Clements and Krolzig (1998), a few studies do focus on the United Kingdom; see Acemoglu and Scott (1994) and Krolzig and Sensier (2000) *inter alia.*

The Markov model is linear within a specific regime, but the model properties differ between regimes. As already discussed, a key feature of the business cycle is negative underlying mean growth of GDP during recessions and positive underlying mean growth during expansions. Although other properties, such as the variance, also may depend upon the regime, a very simple form is taken here, in which only the mean growth rate varies with the regime. That form captures the principal characteristic of interest to us. The Markov model is completed by two probabilities: the probability of remaining in an expansion next period when the economy is in an expansion this period, and the probability of the economy remaining in a recession next period when the economy is currently in a recession. These two probabilities immediately yield the regime-switching probabilities, i.e., the probabilities of moving from an expansion to a recession and from a recession to an expansion. In our basic model, these probabilities are constant for all time periods. In other words, once in an expansion, the probability of switching to a recession in the next period is constant. Similarly, once in a recession, the probability of switching to an expansion is constant.

When estimated using the data on GDP growth, this model indicates an underlying quarterly mean growth rate of +0.76% per quarter during expansions and −0.66% during recessions. When in an expansion, the estimated probability of remaining in an expansion during the next quarter is 96%, which implies a 4% probability of the regime changing to a recession. When in a recession, the estimated probability of remaining in a recession during the next quarter is only 75%, with a corresponding 25% probability of switching to an expansion.[5]

---

[5] Acemoglu and Scott (1994) estimate a similar model for the United Kingdom, obtaining a regime-switching probability and a mean growth for expansions very similar to ours. However, their estimated regime-switching probability and mean growth for recessions differ from ours, perhaps reflecting the different sample periods used and the sensitivity

The estimated probability of switching out of a recession is higher than that of switching out of an expansion because recessions are generally of shorter duration than expansions. That said, the Markov regime-switching model did not utilize any *a priori* dates of recessions and expansions. In estimation, the model itself classifies the observations into expansions and recessions, calculating the regime probabilities without the benefit of any external regime classification.

Figure 7.2a includes the one-quarter ahead forecasts of output growth derived from this nonlinear univariate model. Data up to and including some specific quarter t are used to estimate the model, which then forecasts output growth for the following quarter $t + 1$. During the recession, these forecasts generally are closer to the outcomes than are the forecasts from the linear model, and this Markov model generally predicts output growth to be below average during the recession. Nevertheless, this model largely fails to detect the recession *per se*: the model forecasts a decline in output for only the last quarter of the recession (1992Q2), and even that forecasted decline is virtually zero.

This model also completely fails to predict the onset of the recession. It correctly detects an expansion at the beginning of 1990 and correctly forecasts positive growth for 1990Q2. However, with only a small probability of switching from an expansion to a recession, the model also forecasts strong positive growth for 1990Q3. The onset of the recession in 1990Q3 is as surprising to this model as it is to the simple linear one. For analogous reasons, the recovery is not forecast very well. The forecast growth rates for the six quarters beginning in 1991Q2 hover around zero. The model does not incorporate anything that would enable it to predict the strong positive output growth in 1992Q3.

This section has two immediate implications. Firstly, and most obviously, the conventional univariate linear model cannot capture business-cycle expansion and recession regimes. Likewise, it cannot forecast these regimes.

Secondly, the univariate Markov regime-switching model cannot forecast the onset of the recession or the subsequent recovery either. If this model correctly recognizes period t as being in an expansion (say), the model then predicts a recession in period $t + 1$ with a probability of

---

of the recession estimates to the sample period, given the limited information available on recessions.

(approximately) 4%.[6] In this model's framework, a recession is a rare event. This model does detect the most recent recession once the recession is well underway, and only then does it forecast negative growth. Similarly, recoveries are not forecast—if a recession is recognized for quarter t, the model assigns a constant (and low) probability of 25% to switching to an expansion in quarter $t + 1$. On balance, therefore, the model expects the recession to persist to the next quarter. Thus, while the model may correctly recognize the current regime, it typically does not forecast a change in regime because the model assigns a constant (and relatively small) probability to a change occurring. This model can recognize the current regime—a potentially important feature missing from the linear model—but being able to do so is not in itself of obvious value in forecasting.

For both the linear and regime-switching models, the question now turns to whether explanatory variables can assist in forecasting the business-cycle regimes observed in UK output growth.

7.4 Interest Rates and Output Forecasts

By being univariate, the previous section's models were highly simplistic economically. In almost all realistic economic forecasting models, explanatory variables play an important role, so this section considers model generalizations that include explanatory variables. The usual multivariate linear model assumes that the underlying relationship between the variables is constant over the business cycle. In our case, recessions are explained by the explanatory variables in the equation for output, by negative shocks to that equation, or by some combination of the two. Recessions are forecastable to the extent that the explanatory variables imply predictions of negative growth for output. To avoid having to forecast the explanatory variables themselves, "leading indicator" variables are commonly used, with lags of the leading indicator variables believed to provide predictive information. Thus, current or past observations on such variables are used to forecast future output growth. Other researchers have considered many such variables, but we focus here on short-term interest rates.

---

[6]This estimated probability changes somewhat as additional observations become available.

Not surprisingly, changes in lagged interest rates have a negative effect on output growth in a linear model. In our estimated linear model, changes in the interest rate have statistically significant negative effects on output growth five to seven quarters into the future. Thus, increases in the interest rate tend to dampen output growth over a year later. While a large enough increase in interest rates will necessarily imply forecasting a decline in output, our linear model requires a very large increase in the interest rate—of around three percentage points in one quarter—to generate a forecast of negative growth. Typically, an increase in interest rates just leads to subsequent forecasts of positive growth that are lower than 0.58%, the latter being the forecast of growth in the absence of any change in interest rates. A decline in interest rates likewise leads to a growth rate forecast (five to seven quarters later) above 0.58%. The effect is symmetric: an increase in the interest rate has the same effect on forecast output growth relative to 0.58% as does a decrease of the same magnitude, except that the sign of the effect is switched.

The forecasting performance of this expanded linear model is not impressive over the 1990s recession. Figure 7.2b shows the model's forecasts: negative growth is not forecast for any quarter during the recession. Because the interest rate increased during 1988 and 1989, output growth *is* forecast to be low at the beginning of 1990. For subsequent quarters, however, generally strong growth is forecast, and the linear model does not recognize that the economy is in a recession. While it would be naive to attribute the whole recession to interest-rate changes, Dow (1998, pp. 344–356) does view the increase in interest rates from the middle of 1988 as the trigger that brought on the 1990s recession. In that light, the linear model does not seem capable of capturing the full effects of interest-rate increases on output growth. Furthermore, because the model failed to detect the recession, its forecasts of strong positive growth during 1993 should not be interpreted as forecasts of a recovery from the recession.

The generalized regime-switching model uses information on interest rates in two ways: to detect whether the economy is currently in a recession or an expansion, and to predict the regime for the following quarter. The version of the Markov switching model used here is that of Filardo (1994), in which the probability of remaining in a recession or

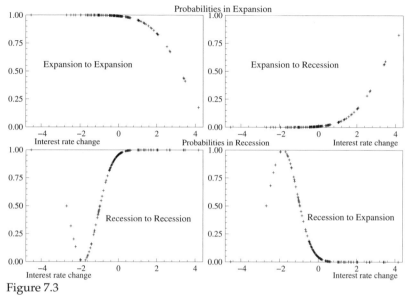

Figure 7.3

Regime-switching probabilities as functions of interest-rate changes.

an expansion (as appropriate) depends on the change in the short-term interest rate. The specific model estimated implies that, if the economy is in an expansion at time t, the interest-rate change of a year earlier influences the probability of the expansion continuing (and hence also of a recession commencing) in period $t + 1$. For a recession at time t, interest-rate changes three quarters earlier influence the regime probabilities in period $t + 1$.

Figure 7.3 plots the estimated effects of interest-rate changes on the regime probabilities for the following quarter $(t + 1)$. In the upper pair of graphs, the economy is in an expansion at time t. The upper left graph (Figure 7.3a) shows the probability of remaining in the expansion, and the upper right graph (Figure 7.3b) shows the probability of switching to a recession. In each case, the points marked on the graph correspond to observed interest-rate changes.[7] From Figure 7.3a, any decrease in the interest rate while in an expansion implies a near-unit

---

[7] The graphs in Figure 7.3 do not segregate expansion and recession observations by the datings discussed in Section 7.2. Rather, all observed interest-rate changes are included in both graphs of a pair (either upper or lower). Also, Figure 7.3 shows the regime transition probabilities as estimated using our entire data sample. For the forecasting exercise,

probability of remaining in the expansion, and hence a near-zero probability of switching to a recession. However, increases in the interest rate shift those probabilities away from one and zero respectively. If the interest rate increases by 1 percentage point (e.g., from 5% to 6%), the expansion probability remains close to unity—around 0.95, or 95%. For an increase of 2 percentage points, the expansion probability declines to around 0.80. For an increase of three percentage points, there is around a 50/50 chance of an expansion or a recession. Thus, declines in the interest rate have no practical effect on regime probabilities during expansions, and increases must be large in order to strongly affect the regime probability.

Interest rates rose steadily through much of 1988 and 1989, with a number of increases of between 1 and 2 percentage points. Although these increases raised the probability of switching to a recession, none were large enough for the regime-switching model to imply a recession as being likely a year later. Thus, even this model fails to predict the onset of the 1990s recession. Once the recession begins, this model does detect it. Because of the prior increases in the interest rate and the observed output declines in 1990Q3–1990Q4, the model forecasts declines in output for 1991Q1–1991Q3; see Figure 7.2b.

The lower graphs in Figure 7.3 show the estimated effects of interest-rate changes on future regime probabilities when the economy is in a recession. Figure 7.3c plots the recession-to-recession probabilities. Temporarily ignoring interest-rate declines of more than 2 percentage points, Figure 7.3c shows that interest-rate changes generally are positively related to the probability of remaining in a recession, and hence are negatively related to the probability of switching to an expansion. This is plausible. A decline of 2 percentage points in interest rates is estimated to give close to a zero probability of remaining in a recession, with smaller declines leading to larger recession probabilities. Unchanged or increasing interest rates imply a near-unit probability of remaining in a recession. Figure 7.3d plots the recession-to-expansion probabilities, which mirror the probabilities in Figure 7.3c.

Figures 7.3c and 7.3d do not have the same simple shapes as the graphs beginning in an expansion. This is because, in practice, the

---

these probabilities are re-estimated each period, using data through only time t when forecasting the regime in time $t + 1$.

chosen mathematical form specifying the functions for recessions was crucial in obtaining economically meaningful results, as discussed in Simpson *et al.* (2001). We believe that a large part of the explanation for this is, yet again, the small number of recession observations in the sample.

The particular functional form employed does, however, result in some anomalies. For example, as Figure 7.3c shows, a decrease in interest rates by 4 percentage points implies (implausibly) a near-unit probability of remaining in a recession. Because changes in the interest rate at a three-quarter lag affect the current regime-switching probabilities for the economy in a recession, the single observed large decline of this magnitude (which occurred early in 1977) is irrelevant in practice. The declines of around 2.5 percentage points, which occurred during the 1970s and early 1980s, are similarly irrelevant for historical recessions; see Figure 7.1d. Thus, the downward slope of left-hand tail in Figure 7.3c seems to facilitate the fitting of the model but can be discounted in terms of its practical implications over the period examined. If this model were used in practice, however, it would be sensible to set the recession-to-recession and recession-to-expansion probabilities to zero and unity respectively for interest-rate decreases of more than 2 percentage points. Doing so would eliminate some potential perverse regime probabilities.

Overall, Figure 7.3 implies that interest-rate changes have a greater effect during recessions than during expansions. Increases in interest rates by up to about 1 percentage point during an expansion have relatively little effect on the probability of remaining in an expansion, whereas a decline of 1 percentage point during a recession substantially alters the probability of remaining in the recession. Policy is complicated further by the lag structure: changes in the interest rate about a year in the past influence current regime probabilities. To return to the 1990s, interest rates actually declined by 1.26 percentage points in 1990Q4. Three quarters later (namely, in 1991Q3), the model predicts a relatively high probability of moving out of the recession in next quarter (1991Q4), with an accompanying forecast of positive growth; see Figure 7.2b. While this forecast was premature, the economy did start growing again in 1992Q3.

Table 7.1

Forecast performance of the four empirical models.

Sample	Univariate models		Models with interest rates	
	linear	nonlinear	linear	nonlinear
	Sign of the growth rate of GDP			
	(quarters correctly predicted/sample)			
Whole period	25/33	26/33	25/33	28/33
Recession	0/8	1/8	0/8	3/8
Expansion	25/25	25/25	25/25	25/25
	MSFE			
Whole period	0,385	0.280	0.332	0.283
Recession	1.233	0.836	1.134	0.892
Expansion	0.113	0.103	0.075	0.088

To summarize, the regime-switching model using interest rates as a leading indicator fails to forecast the onset of the recession, but it does at least later recognize the recession, forecasting negative growth rates one-quarter ahead over 1991Q1–1991Q3. The model is unduly optimistic about a recovery from the recession, forecasting an expansion three quarters too early.

7.5 Measures of Forecast Accuracy

The current section numerically assesses the forecast performance of the four models considered, complementing the previous two sections' graphical and verbal description.

Table 7.1 summarizes the forecasts from the four models, namely, two univariate models and two models using interest-rate information, with a linear version and a regime-switching version considered in each case. The sample period for these calculations is 1990Q1–1998Q1, identical to that in Figure 7.2.

Table 7.1 lists two measures of forecast accuracy. First, Table 7.1 reports how many times the sign of the forecast for the output growth rate matches the assumed sign of the underlying mean growth rate.

For the 8 quarters that Section 7.2 categorizes as being part of the 1990s recession, we assume that the underlying mean growth rate is negative. The remaining 25 quarters of the period are assumed to be in expansion regimes and hence to have positive underlying mean growth rates. For this comparison, only the sign of the output growth forecast is considered (positive or negative). The sign comparison is made using all 33 forecast observations (1990Q1–1998Q1) and also separately for recession and expansion phases within this period.

Second, Table 7.1 reports the mean square forecast error (MSFE) for each model. The MSFE is a conventional statistic for measuring the closeness of forecasts to the corresponding outcomes. In addition to an overall MSFE for each model, Table 7.1 presents MSFEs computed separately for the expansion and recession regimes within this period.

As the first panel in Table 7.1 indicates, the nonlinear regime-switching model using interest rates provides the best forecasts of the sign of output growth in the next quarter. Overall, this model predicts the sign correctly in 28 out of 33 quarters. For the recession, this model correctly forecasts a fall in output for only 3 of the 8 quarters, but the next best model correctly forecasts only 1 quarter out of 8. For the expansions, all models correctly predict positive growth in all 25 periods.

The MSFE error gives a somewhat different and more complex story. Over the whole sample, the univariate regime-switching model obtains the lowest MSFE. It beats both models that use interest-rate information, although the univariate regime-switching model only marginally beats the nonlinear model using the interest rate. For the recession, the nonlinear univariate model produced the most accurate forecasts in terms of MSFE, even while performing relatively poorly in forecasting the sign of output growth. By contrast, the linear model with interest rates obtains the lowest MSFE over the expansions. The nonlinear model using interest rates never has the smallest MSFE.

The value of nonlinear regime-switching models thus may be primarily within recessions, as already noted by Pesaran and Potter (1997), Clements and Smith (1999), and Öcal and Osborn (2000) *inter alia*. Even so, forecasting is still not simple. The nonlinear model with interest rates may provide the best predictions of the sign of GDP growth (and hence of a future recession) without providing the most accurate forecasts in terms of MSFE, even within recessions.

As discussed in Chapter 6, the choice of the best forecasting model may depend crucially on what the forecasts are intended to deliver. One model might be chosen to forecast the direction of change, while another to forecast the growth rate.

7.6 Concluding Remarks

Forecasting economic activity over the business cycle is an exacting task. In particular, because recessions are relatively rare events, we have relatively little information about them and so must be circumspect about the possibilities of accurately capturing their characteristics within a formal statistical model. Nevertheless, regime-switching models with leading indicators offer some hope for forecasting, as the leading indicator can provide predictive information about the future regime. The univariate version of this model is not attractive: it may recognize recessions once they have started, but it contains no mechanism for predicting a switch from an expansion to a recession, or *vice versa*.

We have examined the role of short-term interest rates as a leading indicator for forecasting the 1990s recession in the United Kingdom. This analysis is of current interest, as it highlights the crucial role of interest-rate decisions taken by the Bank of England's Monetary Policy Committee (MPC). Large increases in interest rates substantially raise the probability of switching out of an expansion into a recession. In a recession, less extreme decreases in the interest rate can help initiate a recovery. Even if our model adequately described GDP outcomes, the decisions of the MPC would still be far from simple because changes in the interest rate appear to influence these transition probabilities only a year or so into the future. Setting aside the MPC's principal function of controlling inflation and focusing solely on managing output, the MPC is thus correct to look ahead when it formulates interest-rate policy.

Our results also indicate that there is still much to learn about forecasting the business cycle. In particular, changes in the interest rate alone do not appear to have been sufficient to forecast the onset or length of the 1990s recession, even with the benefit of hindsight. Birchenhall *et al.* (1999) thus develop a procedure for analyzing the role of leading indicators in forecasting the regime, and Birchenhall *et al.* (2001) apply this to the United Kingdom, using interest rates and other financial variables as leading indicators. It still remains to be seen how well the implied composite leading indicator will forecast any subsequent UK recession.

Acknowledgments

This paper was presented by the first author to Section F (Economics) of the British Association for the Advancement of Science at its annual conference in Sheffield, England, September 1999. Computations were performed in the Gauss programming language, Aptech Systems, Inc., Washington; and graphics were generated using GiveWin (see Doornik and Hendry, 2001a). The work discussed in this chapter has grown out of a number of empirical studies with other co-authors at the University of Manchester. We would like to thank Elena Andreou, Mike Artis, Chris Birchenhall, Hans Jessen, and Nadir Öcal for their help in furthering our understanding of modeling economic activity over the business cycle. Financial support from the UK Economic and Social Research Council under grant R000222374 and from the Leverhulme Trust is gratefully acknowledged. Paul Simpson was a PhD student at the University of Manchester when this research was undertaken; he is now employed at the Department for Education and Employment (DfEE), Sheffield.

8 Modeling and Forecasting at the Bank of England

Neal Hatch

Summary

This chapter examines how modeling and forecasting tools are used at the Bank of England to help the Monetary Policy Committee in its policy decisions. Because monetary policy has a delayed effect on output and inflation, a forward-looking approach is essential to inflation targeting, and indeed to monetary policymaking generally.

Economic models are used at the Bank of England for several purposes. Models help the Monetary Policy Committee make its forecasts of output growth and inflation. These forecasts are explicit, not implicit—the Committee's projections are published in the Bank's quarterly *Inflation Report*. Models also aid thinking about monetary policy in other ways, as by simulating the effects of possible changes in the formation of inflation expectations.

8.1 Introduction

This chapter describes how economic models are used at the Bank of England. In 1999, the Bank of England (1999) published details of its suite of economic models. The Monetary Policy Committee (MPC) makes full use of that suite of models in producing its projections for the *Inflation Report* (available at www.bankofengland.co.uk/ir.htm on the Web). In the *Inflation Report*, those projections appear as red and green "fan charts", as they are widely called. This chapter sketches the framework set out in Chapter 1 of the Bank's models book and described in a speech by John Vickers (1999), the Bank's Chief Economist and a member of the MPC. We then consider various examples from the August 1999 *Inflation Report* to illustrate how the models are used.

Economic models are tools to help solve economic problems. A good model achieves clarity by simplifying. By contrast, many economists once thought that it was feasible and desirable to develop more and more complicated models of the economy over time, with those models eventually explaining every facet of the economy. That approach has gone out of fashion, and the recent trend has been towards smaller and more compact models.

Whether a model is good or not depends both on the problem at hand and on how the model is to be used. For example, the MPC needs to use models in their analysis, so the MPC can be thought of as a large-scale consumer of economic models. Quantification, and hence econometrics, are of particular importance for the MPC.

The remainder of this chapter is split into five sections. Section 8.2 describes the role of economic models and forecasts in the MPC's policy process. Then, having explained the "why" and the "how", Section 8.3 provides a few practical examples of the suite-of-models approach used by the Bank of England. Section 8.4 focuses on the properties of the Bank's core model. Finally, Section 8.5 describes some other modeling techniques and information sources that help produce the MPC's projections, and Section 8.6 concludes.

8.2 Models, Forecasts, and Policy

All economic policymakers use forecasts of one kind or another. As the Federal Reserve chairman Alan Greenspan has said:

> Implicit in any monetary policy action or inaction is an expectation of how the future will unfold, that is, a forecast.

Along a similar vein, one former member of the Monetary Policy Committee—Sir Alan Budd—has argued that no valid distinction exists between using forecasts and relying on current observations on the state of the economy, since a forecast is just a transformation of current (and past) observations; see Budd (1998). He also discussed the number of variables used in policy decisions, contrasting the approach of the "hedgehog", who focuses on one or two big things, and the "fox", who watches many things. Thus, hedgehogs may be less likely than foxes to use models in forecasting.

Before considering the roles that models play when the MPC generates its forecasts, it is worth briefly considering two naive (and incorrect) views about how the MPC functions. At one extreme, policy supposedly can be represented by the following simple chain of events:

$$\text{Model} \rightarrow \text{Forecast} \rightarrow \text{Policy.} \tag{8.1}$$

John Vickers (1999) has pointed out that (8.1) errs in several respects. First, (8.1) suggests that models are used in monetary policy only for forecasting. Irrespective of their role in forecasting, models can help understand where the economy has been and how it has behaved. Second, (8.1) implies that forecasts themselves are entirely model-driven, and indeed are driven by a single model. This is not the case, as the previous general discussion of models has already indicated. Third, (8.1) implies that the policy decisions are mechanically driven by forecasts. Models are tools, however, and their use involves judgment.

That said, the left half of (8.1) encapsulates a popular view of the process producing the *Inflation Report* fan charts, in which the MPC:

- brings out the model,
- feeds in the latest economic data,
- presses the button,
- looks at the forecast numbers that are produced, and
- draws the forecast charts.

If the MPC's forecasts really were generated this way, two broad possibilities would be available for policymaking: policy could be decided quite independently of the forecasts, or it could be dictated by the forecasts. In the latter situation, much data that are often mentioned in the minutes of the MPC—such as survey data and reports from the Bank's regional agents—would have little influence, unless the model were incredibly large.

An alternative, "top-down" approach would run like this:

- draw the charts for the projections as desired; and

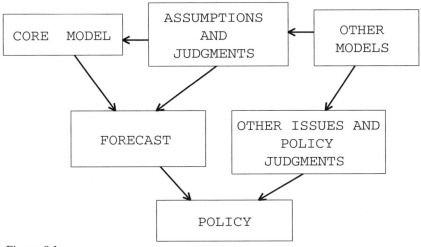

Figure 8.1
The Bank's forecast process.

- make appropriate assumptions and set the equation residuals so that, when the button is pressed, the model produces numbers that match the desired projections.

Neither of these two extreme characterizations resembles the MPC's actual forecast process. The forecast process is rather more complex, as shown in Figure 8.1 above. The remainder of this section discusses who is responsible for the Bank's forecasts, explains how the forecasts are made, and illustrates some of the tools used.

8.2.1 *Whose projections are they?*

Since the MPC was established, the projections in the *Inflation Report* have represented the best collective judgment of the Committee. In particular, those projections are MPC forecasts, rather than Bank staff forecasts.

There is no statutory requirement to publish forecasts. The Bank of England is one of the relatively few central banks that does publish its forecasts: the *Inflation Report* has contained inflation projections since the *Inflation Report* was first published in February 1993, and it has included growth projections since November 1997. The origins of and responsibility for these forecasts must be examined in light of the 1998 Bank of England Act. Section 18 of the Act requires the Bank to publish quarterly reports with:

- a review of monetary policy decisions,
- an assessment of inflation developments in the UK economy, and
- an indication of the expected approach to meeting the Bank's monetary policy objectives.

The Act goes on to say:

> No report under this section shall be published without the approval of the Monetary Policy Committee.

Thus, any forecasts in the *Inflation Report* involve the MPC, at least to the extent that the MPC approves the *Inflation Report* containing them. Furthermore, the *Inflation Report* states:

> Although not every member will agree with every assumption, the fan charts represent the MPC's best collective judgment about the likely path for inflation and output.

How and where individual differences are expressed is in part a matter of degree. MPC minutes are published within a fortnight of each meeting and are one opportunity for members to elaborate upon their differences of view. If differences of view concerning the projections are sufficiently great, the *Inflation Report* can reflect that as well. Indeed, the August 1999 *Inflation Report* was quite explicit that Committee members had somewhat different views, and it explained how alternative assumptions would shift the profile of forecast inflation. This process is still evolving: that *Inflation Report* included a table explicitly showing for the first time how alternative assumptions about variables such as earnings, profit margins, exchange rates, and oil prices might affect the inflation forecast. See the August 1999 *Inflation Report* (p. 53) for further details.

8.2.2 *The forecast process*

The forecast process is intensive. In a typical forecast round, the full Committee has seven meetings to discuss forecast assumptions and risks, with each meeting lasting one-and-a-half hours on average.

As Figure 8.1 indicates, the forecasting process focuses on—but is not limited to—a "core" model. Early in the forecast process, provisional assumptions are made about variables exogenous to the core model. Some assumptions are conventional. For example, the starting point for the exchange rate is taken to be its average over the fifteen working days up to the MPC meeting.[1] Additionally, the short-term interest rate is set at the level that the MPC decides at their meeting prior to the publication of the *Inflation Report*. So, if the Committee decides to change the interest rate at that meeting, the published projections will be consistent with that change. While all such conventions can be discussed and changed by the MPC, they make the process more tractable. There simply isn't enough time to review every assumption in every forecast round.

Let's now turn to some details of how the projections are created. The MPC must decide whether to adjust model equations (as with residual adjustments) in the light of economic news. For example, how should consumer expenditure be viewed if it has been stronger than expected, given income? Should that behavior simply be regarded as random variation—such as measurement error—which will unwind in the next quarter? If so, the profile of expenditure over the next few quarters may be affected, but there would be no long-run consequences for the level of consumer expenditure. If not, should the stronger figures for expenditure be taken to indicate a more permanent shift in the relationship between expenditure and income, relative to the period over which the expenditure equation was estimated? In that case, permanent effects on the level of consumer expenditure could result.

As another example, survey data might suggest a strong outlook for expenditure. How, if at all, should that information be incorporated into the projections? Alternatively, when (e.g.) individuals received windfall payouts arising from the demutualization of some Building

---

[1] There are arguments for using the current spot rate instead, but there are some practical drawbacks to using it in the forecast process.

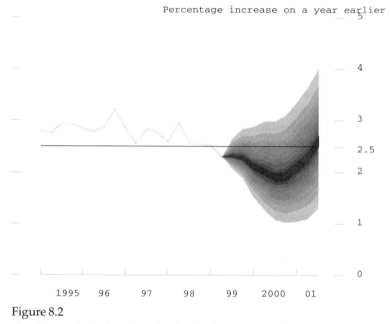

Percentage increase on a year earlier

Figure 8.2
The August 1999 fan chart for the Bank's inflation forecasts.

Societies, how should one have accounted for such an historically rare event, either prospectively or retrospectively? Such questions routinely arise when producing the projections for the MPC. They concern what is happening in the economy, and answering them calls for some economic judgment. Typically, the *Inflation Report* describes the MPC's assumptions on such issues.

When the MPC has agreed on certain key provisional assumptions, Bank staff then start producing a preliminary central projection. Often, doing so raises almost as many questions as it resolves. Far from being a drawback, that represents a great virtue of the resulting iterative process. Throughout the "working back and forth" that then unfolds, much of the discussion and analysis concerns risks and uncertainties.

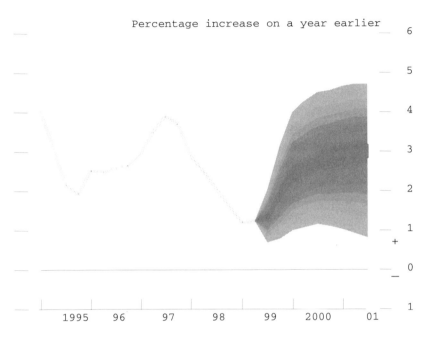

Figure 8.3
The August 1999 fan chart for the Bank's GDP growth forecasts.

The next subsection explains how the *Inflation Report* portrays the forecasts eventually produced and their associated uncertainty.

8.2.3 Fan charts and probabilities

Consider now how the MPC's projections are presented. Since 1996, the Bank of England has published projections in fan charts. These charts try to capture the inevitable uncertainty surrounding the MPC's most likely single projection. They allow the MPC to express judgments about the skewness and variance of the forecast errors, and not just about the central case (i.e., the most likely single outcome). See Chapters 2 and 5 for additional discussion on forecast uncertainty.

Past experience with forecast errors provides the starting point for calibrating the amount of uncertainty, as measured by the variances of projected inflation and output growth.[2] Alternative assumptions for exogenous variables and equation residuals help generate the "skew"—the degree to which the balance of risks is above or below the central projection. The Committee's best collective judgment about the explicitly uncertain prospects for inflation and growth is finally depicted in the fan charts. Views of individual Committee members may differ from that best collective judgment. For example, some individuals may favor alternative assumptions, in which case the *Inflation Report* states that, as happened in August 1999.

To illustrate, Figures 8.2 and 8.3 show the fan charts for RPIX inflation and GDP growth from the August 1999 *Inflation Report*.[3] Both figures are calculated under the assumption that future interest rates are constant at 5.0%. RPIX is the UK retail prices index for all items, excluding mortgage interest payments. The Government's inflation target is defined in terms of RPIX inflation. The current target is 2.5%, as set out in the MPC's remit from the Chancellor; see the August 1999 *Inflation Report* (p. 74). Britton, Fisher and Whitley (1998) and the February 1999 *Inflation Report* (p. 52) explain in more detail how the fan charts are drawn. While no unique way exists for showing this forecast information, using a different method does not alter what is being illustrated: policy is unaffected by how a given probability distribution is drawn.

Figure 8.4 plots the probability distribution for the end of the two-year forecast period in Figure 8.2. The y-axis of Figure 8.4 plots the probability of inflation for 2000Q4–2001Q3 being within 0.05 percentage point of any given inflation rate indicated on the x-axis. For example, in the August 1999 projection round, the probability of inflation being 2.5% (i.e., being between 2.45% and 2.55%) two years later is about 5%. The *Inflation Report* also contains tables listing the MPC's best collective view on the probabilities of inflation and output growth being within certain ranges, given the conditioning assumptions contained

---

[2]The uncertainty actually concerns the forecast error, not the projection on which the latter is based. However, following common usage and for brevity's sake, we talk about the uncertainty of the projection, even although "forecast error uncertainty" is meant.

[3]In the graph format used throughout this chapter, tick marks appear adjacent to the numbers on the right-hand side y-axis. These numbers often are non-negative, so the tick marks should not be mis-interpreted as minus signs.

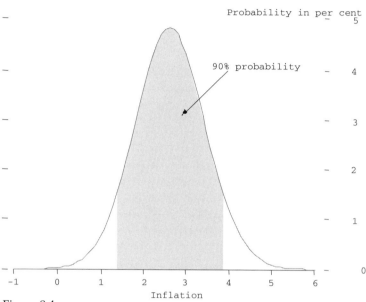

Figure 8.4
The probability of inflation being within 0.05 percentage point of any given inflation rate.

in the *Inflation Report*. The techniques for calculating these probabilities have much in common with non-economic forecasts, such as weather forecasts that give a certain probability of it raining on a particular day.

Other forecasters can and do produce estimates of probabilities for various outcomes of growth and inflation. For example, the National Institute of Economic and Social Research regularly generates similar probability estimates: see Chapter 9. The MPC itself is a consumer of such forecasts. Since the mid-1990s, the Bank has regularly surveyed other forecasters to get their assessment of the probabilities of certain outcomes for inflation and growth.

A section in the *Inflation Report* summarizes the results from that quarterly survey. Figure 8.5 and Table 8.1, both reproduced from the

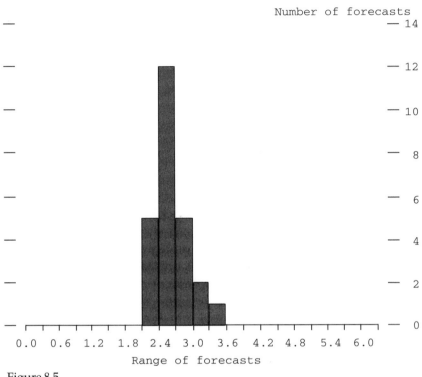

Figure 8.5
The distribution of RPIX quarterly forecasts for 2001Q3.

August 1999 *Inflation Report*, illustrate the type of information available on other forecasters' forecasts. Table 8.1 is based on the reports of 25 forecasters who provided the Bank with their assessment of the likelihood, at three time horizons, of expected RPIX inflation falling in the ranges shown above. This table represents the mean of their responses for each range. For example, on average, forecasters assign a probability of 7% to inflation turning out to be less than 1.5% in 2001Q4.

People often ask what the Bank's forecasting record is, but that question is not easy to answer. It is not sufficient just to look at whether the central projection for inflation was accurate *ex post*. Indeed, it is possible to be "right" for the wrong reason. Likewise, the Bank's projection

Table 8.1
Other forecasters' expectations about RPIX inflation (probability, per cent).

Quarter	Range					
	$<1\frac{1}{2}\%$	$1\frac{1}{2}\%{-}2\%$	$2\%{-}2\frac{1}{2}\%$	$2\frac{1}{2}\%{-}3\%$	$3\%{-}3\frac{1}{2}\%$	$>3\frac{1}{2}\%$
1999Q4	11	25	41	16	5	1
2000Q4	8	15	34	28	9	6
2001Q4	7	12	30	30	13	8

Note: Rows may not sum to 100 because of rounding.

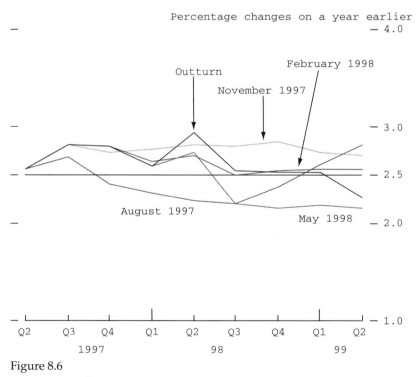

Figure 8.6
Mean RPIX inflation projections and outcomes from the *Inflation Report*.

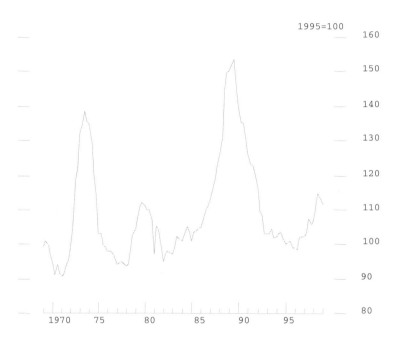

Figure 8.7
The ratio of house prices to earnings.

may differ from the outcome for very good reasons! The economy is hit by many shocks that are (by definition) unknowable before they happen, and these shocks may push the economy off course. The MPC also has only a short history of forecasts. That said, the Bank has published some information about its forecast record, including in a box in the August 1999 *Inflation Report*. Figure 8.6 shows how the MPC's mean projection for inflation evolved between August 1997 and May 1998.

Part of the forecast process includes assessing news and deciding whether the Committee should change its assumptions. The Committee has been quite open about this in the *Inflation Report*, and, on numerous occasions, the Committee has changed its projections in light of new information. For example, in the round for the August 1999 *Inflation Report*, recent evidence led the Committee to change its assumption

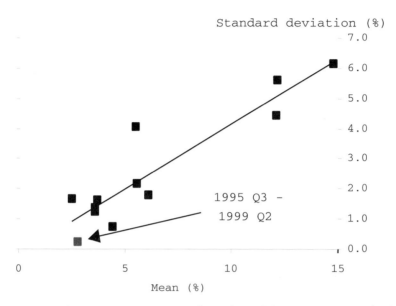

Figure 8.8
The first two moments of annual RPIX inflation.

on future house prices. House prices had previously been assumed to grow in line with nominal earnings. While that remained a sensible long-run assumption, the Committee decided to assume that, over the next two years, house prices would increase at twice the rate of earnings growth in the August round: see Figure 8.7, which plots the ratio of house prices to earnings.

Notably, the overall width of a fan chart is not fixed. The starting point for the width of the fan chart is the distribution of past forecast errors, as discussed above. However, the Committee can and does make assumptions about the width of the fan—through the variance of the probability distribution—if the Committee is more or less certain about some of the components that feed into the projection. In 1998, for example, there was more than usual uncertainty about earnings figures when the Average Earnings Index was suspended, and the width of the fan charts reflected this. Also, as Figure 8.8 indicates, the variability of inflation has fallen over time. The observation indicated by the arrow is for average inflation and its standard deviation over the most recent 16 quarter period. Earlier periods have a higher standard deviation. Inflation may therefore have become slightly easier to forecast, so it is not surprising that the overall width of the inflation fan chart is slightly narrower now than when it was first published in the mid-1990s.

8.3 A Suite of Models

There is no such thing as *the* Bank model. The Bank, like many other organizations, has a suite of models rather than a single model. For producing the MPC's projections, a core model helps ensure overall consistency. For instance, certain forecasts need to "add up", as with the components of domestic demand—consumption, investment, changes in inventories, and government spending. The core model does not function in isolation, however, and its use is tempered by a variety of other models.

Knowledge of the equations in the core model plus the latest data are not sufficient to determine the forecast. Making a forecast relies on a great deal of judgment, much of it based on results from other modeling approaches. For many observers, this is obvious. To others, who are hoping to predict MPC projections by simply studying Bank model equations as published in the models book, this may be disappointing. Furthermore, the core model is not static, and neither is the judgment used in forecasting. The *Inflation Report* documents how modeling assumptions have changed, and how new models are employed to tackle specific issues.

Why is it better to have several models rather than one large model? There are three main reasons, as discussed in the Bank's book describing its suite of models.

First, different problems call for different tools, as Chapter 6 highlights. For example, it is important for the MPC to understand and form a view on the possible macroeconomic effects on the labor market of government policies such as the National Minimum Wage and the Working Families Tax Credit. Typical macroeconomic models are not

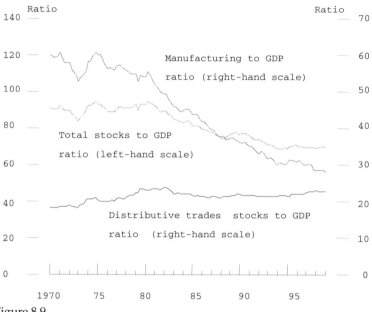

Figure 8.9
Ratios of various inventory measures relative to GDP.

designed to assess those effects, so separate tools must be employed in their analysis, with the results then being integrated into the macroeconomic setting. The *Inflation Report* and the Bank of England's Models book discuss exactly these issues. The Bank has no local monopoly on such activity: for analyzing (e.g.) the Working Families Tax Credit, the Bank drew on research by the Institute for Fiscal Studies.

Second, models are deliberate simplifications. Unfortunately, it is not obvious how far we need to simplify. One good illustration concerns the level of aggregation. Should demand be analyzed as a whole, or split into expenditure components such as consumption and investment? Should consumers' expenditure be broken down into durable and non-durable goods? Should output be analyzed as a whole, or should output for manufacturing and for services be separated? Figures 8.9 and 8.10 show two examples where disaggregation can help

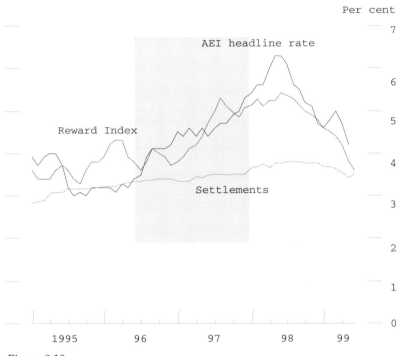

Figure 8.10
Private sector earnings growth and settlements.

understanding of the behaviour of the aggregate, namely inventories and earnings. The Bank also uses highly aggregated Phillips-curve models and small-scale macroeconomic models alongside the more disaggregated macroeconometric core model, highlighting both the aggregation issue and the Bank's pluralist approach to models.

Simplification also bears on the treatment of survey information—for example, of consumer and business sentiment—and of information from the Bank's regional agencies. The core model does not currently utilize these data, whereas the MPC's projections certainly do. Business confidence measures, for instance, are more timely than official output data and are often thought to be a leading indicator of output. The estimated historical relationship between survey responses and output can also provide short-term forecasts for output growth. Although the

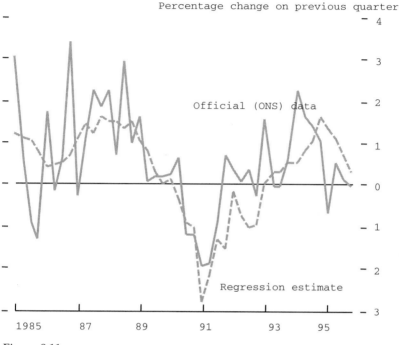

Figure 8.11
Official data for, and survey-based estimates of, manufacturing output.

corresponding forecast errors are typically fairly large, the estimation procedure is more disciplined than simply looking at charts of the data.

These sorts of techniques have been used fairly extensively over the past few years, particularly in light of the significant fall in both business and consumer confidence in the summer and autumn of 1998. The *Inflation Report* discusses much of this work, and technical details appear in the Bank of England's *Quarterly Bulletin*. Figures 8.11–8.14 show some recent examples of the use of survey data at the Bank. Figure 8.11 illustrates how survey data for manufacturing output from the Confederation of British Industry (CBI) can be "mapped" across to the official measure published by the Office for National Statistics (ONS). Figures 8.12, 8.13, and 8.14 show various survey estimates of consumer

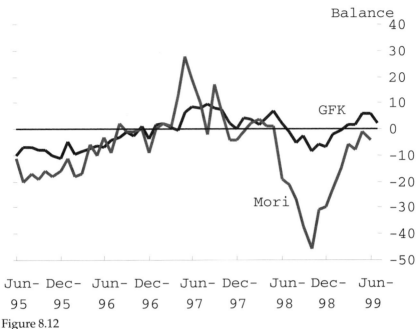

Figure 8.12
Measures of consumer confidence.

and business optimism that can help inform judgments on consumer expenditure, investment, and overall output.[4]

Third, for any given problem and degree of simplification, modeling approaches also differ according to the weight that they place on economic theory. Approaches range from vector autoregressive models to applied theoretical models.

8.4 Properties of the Bank's Core Model

The Bank's core model of the UK economy is a central tool in helping the MPC form its projections for inflation and growth. The core model lies somewhere in the middle of the model spectrum, with its

---

[4]These surveys are from the CBI, the British Chambers of Commerce (BCC), and two research organizations (Mori and Gfk).

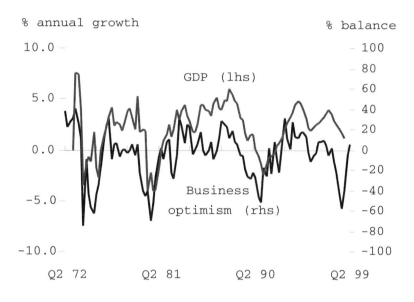

Figure 8.13
CBI business optimism and annual GDP growth.

main properties given by about twenty behavioral relationships. Economic theory plays a much stronger role in determining the model's long-run properties than its short-run dynamics, which are largely data-determined. The model reflects the view of the transmission process outlined by the Monetary Policy Committee (1999). Figure 8.15 sketches how the official interest rate feeds through the model to affect the target variable—inflation. The model is also being continually revised, and it can be operated in several ways.

The core model's key long-run economic properties can be summarized as follows. First, the long-run equilibrium path for real variables—such as output and employment—is independent of the level of prices and inflation. Long-run economic performance depends on the supply side of the economy, and there is no long-run trade-off

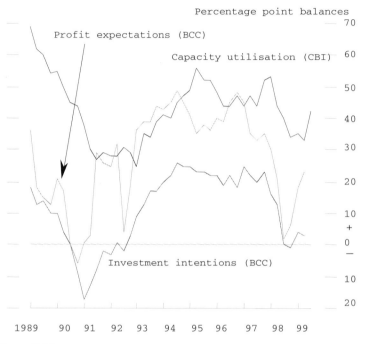

Figure 8.14
Influences on manufacturing investment.

between inflation and unemployment, or between inflation and output. Indeed, high inflation is likely to be damaging to output, employment, and economic welfare more generally, but the core model is not designed to examine these effects.

Second, the price level and inflation depend on monetary policy. Subject to changes in the velocity of circulation, the price level is related to the quantity of money, but money is endogenous unless it is the object of policy choice.

Third, the economy takes time to respond to shocks that perturb it from equilibrium. For example, imbalances between supply and demand cause wages and prices to adjust—but gradually, not immediately. As a result, a short-run trade-off exists between inflation and output: inflation tends to rise or fall according to demand relative to

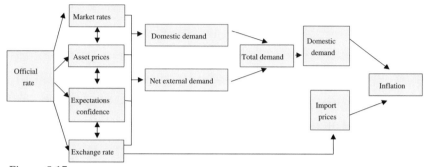

Figure 8.15
A schematic for the monetary transmission mechanism.

the economy's capacity. Many factors affect the nature of this shifting short-run Phillips curve, including the responsiveness of wages and prices to shocks, and expectations about inflation.

Fourth, because the United Kingdom is a small open economy, domestic output and inflation are strongly influenced by the exchange rate and by world trade, output growth, and prices.

8.5   Other Modeling Techniques and Information Sources

Other modeling approaches used at the Bank can be divided into four broad categories: Phillips-curve models, small-scale macroeconometric models, vector autoregressive models, and optimizing models. Each is briefly summarized below, although some have been mentioned already. The Bank of England (1999) contains further details.

Phillips-curve models directly relate price or wage inflation to a measure of real disequilibrium, such as an estimated unemployment or output gap. Though largely data-determined, these models are consistent with a variety of structural models for wage and price determination. These models can be important tools for examining short-run disequilibria.

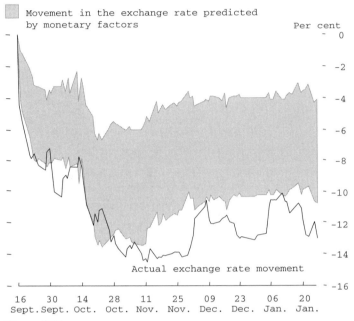

Figure 8.16
News about monetary policy from September 16, 1992 through January 26, 1993.

While Phillips-curve models are typically reduced forms and partial in nature, small-scale macroeconometric models are often complete models of the economy, in the sense that they are self-contained. They are highly aggregated and provide a stylized representation of the whole economy. For example, a small-scale macroeconometric model for an open economy might contain equations for aggregate demand, money demand, a short-run aggregate supply curve, exchange-rate dynamics, and a monetary policy rule. Because these models are small, they are tractable, transparent, and readily used as "test beds".

Vector autoregressive models (VARs) capture statistically the dynamic interactions between a set of variables, so VARs are useful for identifying some key attributes of the data. VARs do not impose strong

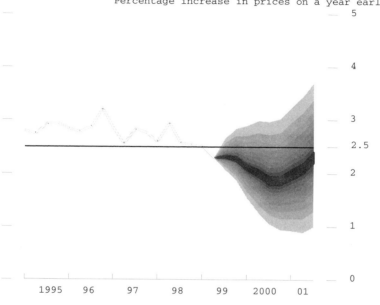

Figure 8.17
The August 1999 projection for RPIX inflation based on market interest-rate expectations.

theoretical assumptions. Structural VARs (SVARs) represent an intermediate approach between basic VARs and more structural economic models, and SVARs have the advantage that they can be used to investigate the effects of shocks on a set of variables.

Optimizing models are often used when we need to investigate the likely consequences of (say) a structural change or economic shock. These models are derived by assuming optimizing behavior of individuals. Such models have been used to investigate the effects of windfall gains arising from the demutualization of Building Societies (also see Ch. 2).

A great deal of our time is also spent looking at analysis and information from outside the Bank, including that from financial markets.

Figure 8.16 illustrates how changes in yield curves can help account for movements in the sterling exchange rate. After the United Kingdom left the Exchange Rate Mechanism (ERM) in 1992, the change in interest rate expectations was consistent with a depreciation of sterling. Also, options on short sterling contracts can be used to produce estimates of the market's probability distribution for short-term interest rates at particular points in the future.

Figure 8.17 shows what the MPC's fan chart for inflation would have been in August 1999, had one used the market's expected path for short-term interest rates rather than the Bank's typical assumption of a constant interest rate. Such information now regularly appears in the *Inflation Report*. It is particularly useful when examining projections by other forecasters, who commonly assume future interest-rate paths that are close to those embodied in the behavior of financial markets.

8.6   Conclusions

In the Bank, as in economics more generally, models are tools to help thinking about economic problems. Their use requires art as well as science, especially when iterating between models, data, and economic judgment.

The Bank uses models for many purposes, which include helping the MPC form its projections for inflation and output growth. While forecasting by committee may be unusual and in some ways difficult, the direct involvement of the MPC in forecasting has important advantages for accountability and for the quality of decision-making.

The Bank uses a suite of models because specific issues often call for new or different tools. It is not possible to construct a single model that will perform all tasks. The Bank's models range in size, complexity, and the role of economic theory. Although a core macroeconometric model helps the MPC make its projections, that model's use depends on various judgments, many of which are informed by other models.

Acknowledgments

The views expressed in this chapter are solely the responsibility of the author and should not be interpreted as reflecting the views of the Bank of England or the Monetary Policy Committee.

9 Forecasting the World Economy

Ray Barrell

Summary

This chapter focuses on the problems of endemic structural change, the importance of using a structural econometric model to interpret such changes, and the consequent role of judgment when forming forecasts. Empirical illustrations highlight these themes through unexpected structural changes involving both deteriorations to and improvements in economic conditions. Recent deteriorations include the East Asian crisis in 1997 and 1998, the changing structure of capital flows, and the collapse of the Long Term Capital Management (LTCM) hedge fund in September 1998. Improvements include effects from living in a low-inflation world, and the associated reduction of inflation uncertainty in the United Kingdom.

9.1 Introduction

Economic forecasting is an important tool for academic economists who want to influence the policy debate. There is a great deal of interest in what might happen in the next quarter or in the next year, with many commercial forecasters filling that need. Academic forecasters have a more distinctive role. They produce forecasts that are more firmly based in economic analysis, and they ask conditional questions about the future such as:

What will happen next quarter (or next year) *if* the government does this, or *if* the markets do that?

They also discuss the uncertainty surrounding forecasts. For instance, the UK's National Institute of Economic and Social Research (hereafter, the "Institute") publishes forecasts and their standard errors in its quarterly *National Institute Economic Review*. The Bank of England has also recently started publishing confidence intervals for its predictions of UK inflation and GDP growth; see Chapters 5 and 8. As background to forecasting in an uncertain environment, this introductory section reviews various roles that economic models play in forecasting and policy analysis. The remainder of this chapter then examines endemic structural change and forecast uncertainty and shows how the Institute's forecast models have helped address these issues.

Economic models are probably the best tools around which to organize a forecast. They typically involve the estimation of statistical relationships for major economic variables, and they may cover many markets in the economy, albeit in an aggregate way. Such models also can help organize ideas and embed the relevant economic theory. Because a well-constructed model summarizes the economy in the way that the researcher thinks that the economy functions, that model is also a testing ground for economic theories. The overall behavior of the model can be informative about its underlying assumptions. A good model also provides a way for organizing projections through internal consistency and consistency with the past. See both Chapters 3 and 8, which detail this approach to modeling and forecasting.

To produce good forecasts and policy analyses, a model must have certain characteristics. The following items serve as a checklist for modelers generally:

- the model should have long-run equilibria,
- stabilizing feedbacks should ensure that the equilibria are attained,
- the dynamics of adjustment in response to shocks must be realistic,
- all relevant variables should be parsimoniously but completely covered, and
- there must be a sensible description of behavior in reaction to expected events.

On the last item, expectations are central to the analysis of many current events. In financial markets, exchange markets, and probably labor markets, it is convenient to assume that people form consistent expectations about the future when making decisions. This assumption is problematic in forecasting, as it normally requires that the forecaster assume that others in the economy agree with the forecast and are expecting it to happen. Otherwise, the forecaster needs to reconcile the forecast with the (presumably incorrect) expectations held by others. The Institute's *Review* for July 1999 discusses these problems in depth for the UK economy and its potential for membership in the EMU.

Forecasts—or rather, the resulting forecast errors—are inherently uncertain, so producers of forecasts should report the confidence intervals around forecasts. That said, many forecasters fail to do so, as they use *ad hoc* forecasting methods or rely on catchy headlines to justify their existence. While confidence intervals are often lacking in practice, they are still important to calculate, as they emphasize the uncertainty inherent to forecasting. Decomposing uncertainty by source may also be useful, as with the relative importance of exchange-rate uncertainty, and as with sources of uncertainty within the economy, such as consumption uncertainty relative to investment uncertainty. Model-based forecasts in academic institutions are thus central to a healthy policy debate, especially when the latest developments in economics can be taken on board while looking at current world events. Moreover, knowledge can be accumulated in the models themselves through both academic research and policy analysis.

The Institute uses its models for quarterly forecasts and for policy analysis. The Institute's world model NiGEM ("National Institute Global Econometric Model") is widely used by central banks and finance ministries for both purposes, so it must pass "market" tests as well as academic evaluations. NiGEM covers all OECD countries individually and all non-OECD countries individually or in blocks. We have found it essential to have a theoretically coherent forecasting model that produces a long-horizon forecast. Academic research also helps monitor and evaluate these forecasts—a particularly important role when the world is evolving and changing.

A taxonomy of shocks to the economy is useful when looking at forecasts. Shocks are typically either large and infrequent or small and frequent. They can be exogenous to the economy, in that they are driven by outside random forces; or they can be the result of conscious decisions by policymakers. Forecasters tend to focus on big shocks, such as German re-unification and the East Asian crisis. However, all economic relationships are subject to uncertainty, and that uncertainty is important when interpreting forecasts.

The past pattern of unexplained changes can help measure forecast uncertainty. Forecast models can also help investigate the sources of uncertainty. For example, if we knew the path of UK exchange rates, we would be more certain about the future path of UK inflation. Models provide one of the few ways to examine such uncertainty clearly. To illustrate, in NiGEM, 95% of all possible outcomes for UK inflation should fall within one percentage point of the mean UK inflation forecast if sterling is fixed to the Euro. That would make the UK government's inflation target easy for the Bank of England to achieve. Currently, however, the UK exchange rate can move freely, and it sometimes does so without much apparent reason. Allowing for a floating exchange rate in NiGEM increases uncertainty about inflation by 20%. Inflation might then sometimes overrun its target bounds: a sudden drop of 10%–15% in the exchange rate is possible, and that would raise inflation by 1–2 percentage points per annum within the year.

Major economic changes may be difficult to anticipate, but a well-established research and modeling team can analyze such developments. Two examples of such changes are the 1997–1998 collapse of the East Asian economies and the unexpectedly strong growth rate of the US economy from 1996 to 2000. Both may represent fundamental structural changes in the way those economies work. The Institute had undertaken work on the East Asian countries and their exchange rates before the crisis developed, and hence there was a framework within which to work; see Barrell, Anderton, Lansbury and Sefton (1998) and Barrell and Pain (1998). Also, NiGEM has a fully specified model of the US economy and, for some time, we have been modeling structural change and the possibilities of a technological revolution; see the Institute's May 1999 *Review*.

The next section (Section 9.2) examines endemic structural change. That sets the scene for Sections 9.3–9.8 which consider in more detail six specific structural changes from the last two decades to highlight how the Institute's models have helped analyze and interpret events in European labor markets, Japanese consumers' expenditure, the East Asian financial crisis, and the collapse of LTCM in 1998, as well as low inflation and its changed uncertainty in the United Kingdom. Section 9.9 concludes.

9.2 Endemic Structural Change

Endemic structural change is common, and we have been looking for such change in our model construction for over a decade. Identifying historical breaks is a first step to utilizing our knowledge of past developments.[1] If we know when the changes occurred, we can look for them with statistical techniques that condition on knowing the breakpoints. However, we do not always know the timing of the changes involved, and then we need to utilize other methods of analysis.

Structural change may occur for many reasons. Governments are an obvious reason, as they frequently try to influence economies in order to improve their performance. For instance, the process of European integration has altered patterns of location and trade, and multi-country models that ignore European integration would miss many interesting developments in the last 20 years. Structural change also can arise almost by accident, as with the collapse of the Soviet Union. That collapse inevitably altered the structure of Europe, so we have to model these changes.

While models can be useful for capturing structural change, judgment may play a role as well, particularly when constructing model-based forecasts. The East Asian crisis and the New Economy in the United States highlight the role of judgment when making forecasts. Accurate forecasts may need to rely on judgments about structural change. Because change is endemic, historical data are typically drawn from several regimes. Consequently, if we do not make judgments about future changes but rely solely on statistical analyses of the past, we may obtain biased forecasts that are contaminated by the effects of several different regimes.

---

[1] Our discussion of structural change is closely related to the concepts in Clements and Hendry (1999, Chapter 7), where they discuss a taxonomy of forecast errors.

To illustrate concretely the roles of both models and judgment in economic forecasting, we examine six case studies: European labor markets (Section 9.3), Japanese consumers' expenditure (Section 9.4), the recent East Asian financial crisis (Section 9.5), the collapse of LTCM (Section 9.6), the current low-inflation economic environment (Section 9.7), and forecast uncertainty for UK inflation (Section 9.8).

9.3 European Labor Markets

European labor markets have experienced major changes over the last two decades. In the 1980s, the *Scala Mobile* gradually disappeared in Italy, and the Netherlands introduced the 1982 Wassaner agreements on competitive devaluation by wage moderation.

More widespread changes occurred in the early 1990s. Re-unification fundamentally altered Germany. UK labor markets became more efficient, and the UK equilibrium unemployment rate fell. Change in Italy continued; and Spain, France, and Denmark also saw some evolution. Sweden and Finland reformed their labor markets, and wage behavior changed, such that their measured equilibrium unemployment rates rose. Without accounting for these changes, we cannot sensibly analyze the prospects for growth and inflation in Europe, and we cannot discuss European integration.[2]

To illustrate, Figures 9.1 and 9.2 plot past unemployment rates and our model-based projections thereof for Germany, Finland, and Sweden. The historical data highlight the magnitude of the structural changes that occurred. German re-unification caused a major structural change in German labor markets, and effects from the addition of a differently trained workforce will only slowly disappear in Germany. This is, of course, a judgment, although Franz and Steiner (2000) provides some support for this view: work experience in the East German labor market does not appear to affect post-unification productivity.

In the early 1990s, both Finland and Sweden underwent major crises, including banking crises and exchange rate problems in 1992,

---

[2]Several studies from the Institute have monitored structural changes in European labor markets, and we first discussed such change in 1990. Anderton and Barrell (1995) examines the ERM and European labor markets, and Barrell (1994) surveys the work (then) to date for the United Kingdom. More recent studies include Morgan (1996a, 1996b), Barrell and Morgan (1996), and Barrell and Dury (2001).

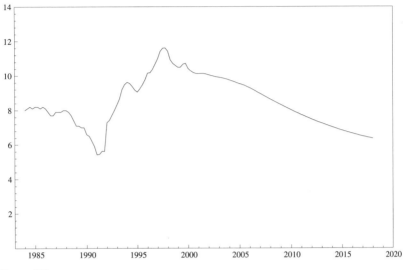

Figure 9.1
The German unemployment rate.

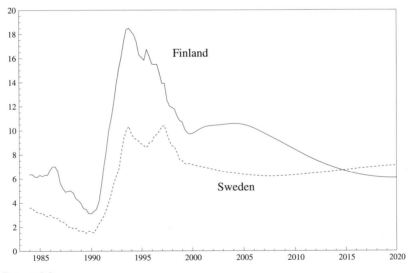

Figure 9.2
Swedish and Finnish unemployment rates.

and mounting taxes to finance generous welfare systems. The Finns were also badly hit by the collapse of Russian trade in 1992. Both Finland and Sweden reformed their labor markets, raising the sustainable unemployment rate. As the projections in Figure 9.2 indicate, we think that these shifts will be long-lasting because the structure of these economies and their social benefit systems have changed.

Sometimes we learn by example from other countries, rather than undertake econometric work. For instance, we made some allowance for the New Deal in the United Kingdom, basing the adjustments on experiences in countries such as Denmark, where a similar program of reforms began in 1994; see Barrell and Genre (1999).

9.4 Japanese Consumers' Expenditure

Not all structural changes can be quickly detected or modeled by econometric methods, and judgment again plays a role. The behavior of recent Japanese consumers' expenditure illustrates.

The events in East Asia in 1997 were complex, and one of the more important events went almost unnoticed because of currency turmoil. The Japanese had been liberalizing their financial markets, and in the autumn of 1997 pension funds had to clarify their balance sheets, which revealed that they did not have enough funds to pay all of their commitments in full. Japanese consumers reacted strongly to this news, and savings rose. The decline in consumers' expenditure slowed down the economy by as much as did the currency turmoil, and the former has more important long-term implications.

We had to make judgments about this event in our forecast, as discussed at length in the Institute's April 1998 *Review*. We decided to set a negative "residual" of -1.5% on our equation for Japanese consumers' expenditure for the immediate future to take account of the problem and ensure that savings would be higher. In our estimated equation, expenditure depended in the long run on personal disposable income and real net financial wealth, with relative weights of 0.9 and 0.1. The equation was in equilibrium correction form—if expenditure is not at its long-run equilibrium level, it "corrects", albeit slowly. Our data on financial wealth did not include the position of pension funds as perceived by consumers, and hence would not have explained

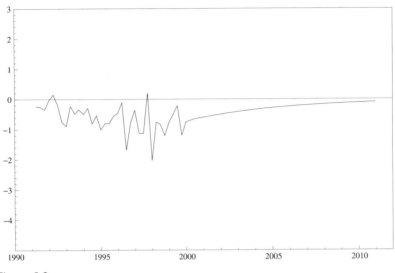

Figure 9.3
Residuals for the equation of Japanese consumers' expenditure.

the consequent rise in savings. Figure 9.3 plots the equation's residuals through the end of 1998 and our forecast judgment from the July 1999 baseline. Our judgment was well-founded for 1998.

9.5   The East Asian Financial Crisis, 1997–1998

The *world* economy is subject to major structural shocks as well, and models should be able to deal with these. The shocks to East Asia in 1997 were very large, and the collapse of exchange rates in East Asia appeared to be leading the world economy into a major slowdown. It did not—and, based on our models, we did not think it would—although most commercial forecasters did. The collapse in East Asia arose from a major reversal of capital flows, which changed by more than $100 billion between 1996 and 1997. Forecasting a year or two ahead with some models, it looked as though world trade would collapse and the world economy would slow down.

A theoretically coherent model with forward-looking financial markets gave us a different, less pessimistic result. The financial capital had to go somewhere else, and hence the market and prices would have to adjust. Because the balance of saving and investment had changed, our model's solution for a longer horizon (20 years) included a lower path for real interest rates in the OECD. In a coherent model with forward-looking expectations, the long-term interest rate therefore had to fall, as it in fact did. Likewise, the model predicted the (actual) strengthening in the equity market. The automatic stabilizers of the market worked. We could predict these adjustments early on because the tools were in place to do so. By contrast, many commentators ignored the role of automatic stabilizers and so forecast a sharp slowdown in the OECD. The OECD's *Economic Outlook* for December 1997, for instance, analyzed the crisis with the assumption that real interest rates would remain constant.

Work on the East Asian economies, cited above, suggested that their currencies were only slightly overvalued. We believed that the economies would respond rapidly and strongly to the devaluation. After some initial problems, many of those economies have indeed recovered strongly. In 1999Q2, output in South Korea was 9.8% higher than a year previously. Taiwan and Singapore, which were less affected by a falling exchange rate, each grew by about 6.5%. Chinese output grew by 7.1%; and Thailand, Malaysia, and the Philippines also grew, albeit more slowly. Only Indonesia was in the doldrums, but mainly for political reasons not directly associated with the crisis.

The events in East Asia were only a minor problem for OECD economies. The money flowing into East Asia dried up, but it had to go somewhere else. The stabilizing forces of the market worked, reducing long-term borrowing costs in the OECD. The extra capital could only be absorbed if saving fell and investment rose in the long run. Financial markets knew this, and long-term interest rates fell and equity markets strengthened. Financial wealth rose, increasing consumers' expenditure. Many forecasters looking a year or so ahead missed this shock-absorbing mechanism.

Using models with forward-looking expectations in financial markets, Institute forecasters stressed the self-stabilizing nature of a market economy. They analyzed the effects of the change in capital flows using NiGEM, which indicated that long-term interest rates would fall. In NiGEM, this fall in interest rates offset most of the trade shock, closely paralleling actual world events in 1998. Barrell, Dury, Holland, Pain and te Velde (1998) provide a more fully developed position on the East Asian crisis. A sequence of events occurred, and a well-specified model helped peel away the layers of events and separate the effects of falling commodity prices from those due to changes in trade.

9.6   The Collapse of LTCM in 1998

Forecasters have their successes as well as their failures, especially when policymakers respond to their forecasts, as the history of the LTCM hedge fund highlights. In September and October 1998, the world stood on the brink of a major financial disaster due to the collapse of the prominent hedge fund, Long Term Capital Management (LTCM). The possible outcomes for the world economy depended on what might happen to the US banking system. The Institute forecast assumed that policy would prevent a collapse of the banking system.

As background, by the summer of 1998, the East Asia crisis had been weathered, but more currencies were moving sharply. The Russian ruble collapsed, and the Russian government defaulted on its sovereign debt. There also was pressure on Brazil, which held off until January 1999. Suddenly, the international banking system looked exposed. European and American banks had lost a great deal of money in East Asia and Russia, and they were short of capital. Public-sector banks in Germany and France had been particularly exposed, but they were backed by their taxpayer owners. Banks adjusted their balance sheets, reducing the riskiness of their loan portfolios. Some banks reduced their overall level of loans, so capital markets began to contract.

When LTCM collapsed in late September 1998, there was a severe risk of cumulative financial failure. Two possible outcomes seemed likely: either financial markets would survive, and nothing would happen; or they would collapse, changing the whole world. The Institute forecast could be described as bimodal, with the most likely mode being survival. We thought that this mode covered 60% of the distribution, with 40% allocated to the mode involving financial crisis and the collapse of aggregate demand.[3]

---

[3] See Barrell, Dury, Holland, Pain, N. and te Velde (1998) which was first presented at various conferences in September 1998, including at a meeting in Vienna on the day that

Fortunately, policy altered and the crisis was avoided. The policy adjustment involved a monetary easing that lowered interest rates and stimulated equity markets. That in turn increased inflationary risks, but those risks appeared well worth taking at the time. Even so, those policy actions may have created future risks: we have been living in a low-inflation world for several years now, but it is not clear how long we will continue to do so.

9.7   Living in a Low-inflation World

One current challenge to modelers and forecasters is to explain why we now live in a low-inflation world, after experiencing (typically) much higher inflation rates during the 1970s and 1980s. Some say that inflation has been low because US productivity increased particularly rapidly, with no emergence of capacity constraints. While US unemployment rates have been well below most estimates of long-run sustainable levels, perhaps the US labor market has changed and potential output risen. Structural change of this sort could keep inflation below expected levels for a few years. This section thus examines US labor markets, the strong dollar, and US productivity as potential explanations for the current low-inflation environment.

As Figure 9.4 shows, both US inflation and unemployment rates have fallen during the 1990s. This joint behavior is unusual, and it is common to assume that the world must be changing in order for this to happen. Standard economic theory suggests that inflation should increase when the unemployment rate falls below its long-run sustainable level, which might also be the long-run average if markets work well and do not change too much. The US unemployment rate is at a historically low level, yet there appears to be no pressure on the economy or on the price level. However, asset prices are very high, and excess demand for goods may have spilled over into asset markets.

All that said, little evidence exists to support any supposed changes in the US labor market. Rather, strong demand and a strong exchange rate appear primarily responsible. The strength of the dollar has held down consumer price inflation while allowing producers to raise their

---

LTCM collapsed.

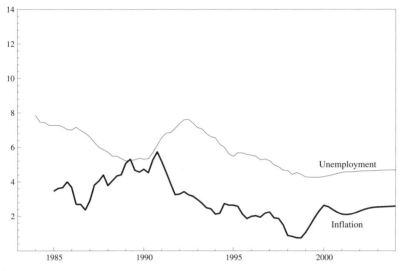

Figure 9.4
US unemployment and inflation rates (forecast values are plotted from 1999).

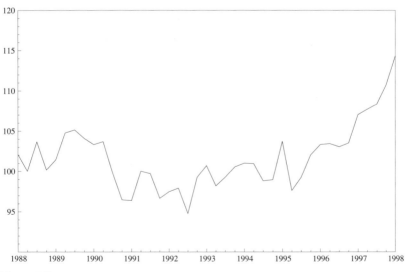

Figure 9.5
The US real effective exchange rate.

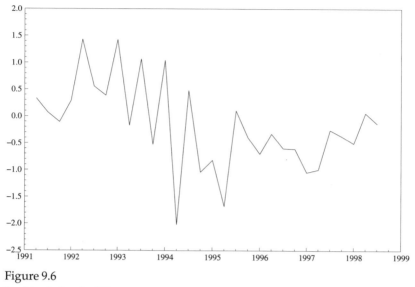

Figure 9.6
Residuals for the US wage equation.

prices. Consequently, the US current account deficit has sharply increased, and its current level may not be sustainable in the long run. Figure 9.5 plots the US real effective exchange rate: it is hard to find good fundamental reasons for its steady rise over the late 1990s.

Equation residuals can help in determining whether the behavior of the labor market has shifted significantly. Our estimated (forward-looking) wage equation fits well, as can be seen from its residuals, which are plotted in Figure 9.6. This equation relates the growth of the real producer wage (measured as compensation per person-hour, deflated by the output deflator at factor cost) to the deviation of the real producer wage from longer-term productivity. This equilibrium correction term is mediated by the effects of unemployment, and the equation is dynamically homogenous in forward-looking and backward-looking rates of changes in prices.

This wage equation does over-predict in the early 1990s and underpredict in the mid-1990s. However, from 1997 onwards, the equation appears to be approximately on track. Our labor-demand equation is also on track. We thus do not find evidence for changes in labor market structure. Rather, the strong dollar reduced consumer prices, thereby increasing the real wages that consumers receive and making them more willing to work. Employment has risen. This wedge should be temporary. If the exchange rate falls, inflation could re-emerge, as some evidence suggests is happening for 2000.

Nevertheless, our models might miss a change in the US labor market. We have to make a judgment about this in our forecast, and our projection for the United States will be heavily influenced by such a decision. Some of our reasoning about US labor markets goes as follows.

US labor productivity grew at 1% per year over 1975–1995, whereas it grew at 2% per year over 1996–1998. Over the latter period, employment grew by more than 1% per year—remarkably strong, but possibly the result of strong output growth.

Over 1993–1998, the capital stock rose by 13%, a very large increase. Additionally, capital productivity rose by 1% per year over 1996–1998, compared to 0.4% per year on average over the previous 20 years. Such strong growth in productivity, accompanied by strong growth in factor usage, is unusual. Indeed, demand curves for factors appear to be shifting outward for some reason, rather than labor supply shifting down the labor-demand curve. The latter would be implied if structural change in the sustainable unemployment rate was the cause of low inflation in the United States.

From 1997 through the end of 1999, the strength of the US stock market has surprised many people. It is widely believed that changes in US technology and equity prices are strongly linked. As the numbers above suggest, the United States may be undergoing a productivity miracle—perhaps a computer-based revolution. This effect is not easily detected in the labor market because technical progress may be capital-augmenting, thus affecting production in a different way from that normally associated with changes in technology. If so, then profits should grow more rapidly, and the equity market should boom.

If the technological revolution is largely in the United States, that country's resulting ability to produce more and better products should imply a stronger real exchange rate. The evidence fits together to produce a story about a productivity miracle, but the question remains: why doesn't the miracle spread to other countries? Perhaps unglobalized parts of the service sector are involved. Alternatively, the computer-based revolution appears heavily dependent on the English language: hence this revolution should spread first to other Anglophone countries. Notably, Australia and Ireland have recently experienced rapid growth; and the UK unemployment rate has fallen to a low level, while inflation has been low and output has been at or above capacity. Perhaps there is a commonality here.

This is a very seductive story, but how strong is the evidence for it? Can our models and intellectual structures produce alternative explanations for what we see? The answer is—yes, there are other potential explanations. At best, we might say that the United States has become more efficient. This more circumspect view is important, because it could imply that the stock market is overvalued, and that the strong dollar has held inflation down. A weakening of the dollar and a fall in the stock market could bring both rising inflation and falling demand. Indeed, the OECD's December 1999 *Economic Outlook* sees this combination as the major risk facing the world economy, and it analyzes at some length the consequences of a decline in asset prices.

9.8   Inflation Uncertainty in the United Kingdom

The uncertainty associated with forecasts can oftentimes be as important information as the forecasts themselves. That said, forecast uncertainty is hard to analyze for the financial crises of 1997–1998 and for the US equity price increases of the late 1990s—fortunately, few shocks are so large as these. In analyzing forecast uncertainty, past patterns of equation residuals are typically used to construct confidence intervals for forecasts, and couterfactual simulations can help sort out the major sources of uncertainty. This section thus describes how NiGEM helps evaluate forecast uncertainty—specifically, the forecast uncertainty of a politically prominent economic variable, inflation. We first discuss the mechanics of calculating forecast uncertainty; then we examine how different policy rules can affect the forecast uncertainty of inflation. Barrell, Dury and Hurst (2001) discusses the basic framework; further details appear in NIESR (1999), available from the Institute. See Clements and Hendry (1999) for details on stochastic simulation.

Models provide almost the only way to examine forecast uncertainty clearly, as our use of NiGEM illustrates. To estimate forecast uncertainty, we calculate the historical shocks to all of NiGEM's (approximately) 1000 estimated relationships. We then draw future "representative" shocks from a set of historical shocks, where that set spans 1993Q1–1997Q4 on the assumption that the near future will be similar to the near past. The model was constructed so as to account for some known structural changes. In general, we assume that the model applying to the recent past is structurally similar to that for the future, whereas the more distant past may represent a set of different regimes: shocks from that past would have to be drawn carefully.

By repeatedly applying the historical shocks to our forecasts, we produce a set of new "future histories". The shocks are applied sequentially to the 20 quarters over 1999Q1–2003Q4, running the model "forward" for each quarter's shocks to calculate the expectations that would be a reasonable response to that quarter's news. This forward calculation alters expectations of all variables in the shocked quarter. Then, shocks are applied to the next quarter, with the previous quarter's changes reflected in the baseline. This exercise is repeated sequentially to all 20 quarters; and each of these trials is replicated more than 200 times, using different sequences of historical shocks each time.

This whole exercise is performed twice, once with and once without shocks to the exchange rate. Because exchange rates in the model follow a forward-looking open-arbitrage condition, they can "jump" with news. Long-term interest rates are the forward convolution of expected future short-term interest rates, so the former can also jump in the first period. These rational-expectations elements are augmented by labor-market relationships that look both forward and backward. For each OECD economy, NiGEM includes a supply side, a demand side, and a set of asset-accumulation relationships, including government-sector, foreign-sector, and private-sector financial accounts.

From such stochastic simulations of our structural models, we can construct forecast-error confidence intervals. These can be calculated for different monetary policy feedback rules, as discussed in Barrell *et al.* (2001). The remainder of this section compares the calculated forecast uncertainty for three possible interest-rate feedback rules: monetary targeting, inflation targeting, and a combined rule.

We first assume that the policymaker simply targets a nominal monetary aggregate and changes interest rates when the observed nominal aggregate diverges from its target. The German Bundesbank ostensibly used this form of policy rule before the European Monetary Union. The United Kingdom also adopted rules of this form in the 1980s.

As an alternative, we consider pure inflation targeting, as characterized by recent policy at the Bank of England. If inflation exceeds its target, then the interest rate is raised, and inflation will eventually subside. The speed at which the Bank reacts is very important. If the feedback coefficient is relatively large in the targeting rule (which we must see as an abstraction from the actual decision making process), then the policymaker may actively move interest rates when inflation looks as if it will diverge from target. The Bank appears to do so, as discussed in the Institute's October 1999 *Review*. See also Chapter 8, which describes the Bank's approach to modeling, forecasting, and policy in detail.

Finally, these two pure targeting rules can be compared to a combined rule—such as the European Central Bank claims to be using—in which the authorities adjust the interest rate in response to multiple target discrepancies, such as for a monetary aggregate and for inflation. If the nominal aggregate deviates from its trend (the reference value for the broad money measure M3 in Europe), then the policymaker adjusts the interest rate. Likewise, the policymaker adjusts the interest rate if inflation is outside its target range.

Figures 9.7 and 9.8 plot 95% confidence intervals for the UK inflation forecast under the three different policy rules. The confidence intervals look relatively flat for much of the future, after the effect of current information dies away. The policy rule in place may affect the degree of forecast uncertainty, and hence the width of the forecast confidence interval. Together, Figures 9.7 and 9.8 show that the confidence interval narrows slightly when moving from a credible monetary aggregate regime through a credible mixed targeting regime to pure inflation targeting. *Credible* policies must be stressed in this analysis: if the authorities are not seen as credible, the confidence intervals around the forecasts could be much wider.

Other variations in targeting rules could also be considered. If the Bank should try to look too far forward, that could increase forecast uncertainty, as explained in Blake (2000). While Figures 9.7 and 9.8 suggest that changing the policy rule itself may not greatly reduce forecast

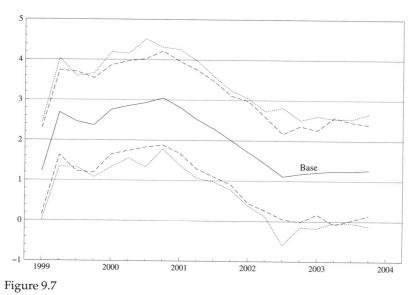

Figure 9.7

95% confidence intervals for UK inflation under money-stock targeting (dotted line) and under a combined money-and-inflation rule (dashed line).

uncertainty in a forward-looking world, our analysis may fail to capture other possible gains, such as from making the Bank independent.

That said, exchange-rate stability does imply a large reduction in forecast uncertainty, especially for a small open economy like the United Kingdom. The variability of the UK inflation rate—as measured by its root mean square error (RMSE)—both with and without shocks to the exchange rate, reveals that shocks to the exchange rate increase this measure of inflation uncertainty by 20%. The exchange rate is clearly a major policy concern for the United Kingdom, and these results suggest that fixing it would reduce the volatility of inflation.

From our analysis, 95% of all possible outcomes for UK inflation should fall within one percentage point of the mean forecast if sterling is fixed to the Euro. This could make the UK government's inflation target easy for the Bank of England to achieve. Currently, however, the UK exchange rate is floating. The real UK exchange rate has had some large, infrequent, sudden jumps, as in 1992 (downwards) and in 1996 (upwards). Our stochastic simulations include these shocks, which are

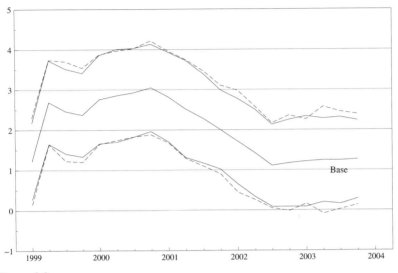

Figure 9.8
95% confidence intervals for UK inflation under a combined money-and-inflation rule (dashed line) and under an inflation-targeting rule (solid line).

the source of most of the increased uncertainty. However, the UK real effective exchange rate has been relatively constant since 1997. The recent stability of the exchange rate at a relatively high level may partly explain why inflation has stayed well within its 95% confidence interval in the late 1990s. In our stochastic simulations, those large exchange-rate shocks are occasionally applied to replications, causing more variation in simulated inflation than recently observed. We think this is reasonable, as the exchange rate could suddenly drop by 10%–15%, increasing inflation by 1–2 percentage points per annum within the year, and pushing inflation well outside its target range.

With NiGEM, we can calculate confidence intervals for output, prices, and inflation in the United Kingdom, the United States, and Europe under different hypothesized circumstances. Consequently, we can investigate the effects of a policy rule on forecast uncertainty and evaluate whether such effects are important. The treatment of the exchange rate is central to our analysis. Exchange-rate uncertainty contributes substantially to inflation uncertainty in a small open economy such as the United Kingdom, and less so in large open economies such as the United States and Europe. That said, treating the European exchange rate stochastically creates a conceptual problem: the Euro was created only recently, and we do not know how it would have behaved in the past. To address this problem, we looked at the past shocks faced by the core European countries and applied those shocks to the Euro bilateral exchange rate with the dollar. The overall results differ from the past, and the constructed shocks must be seen as synthetic, but they may well characterize the future.

9.9 Conclusions

Large structural models are useful to forecasters, and they allow academic modelers to produce coherent frameworks for policy analysis. Such model-based forecasts are central to government policy analysis and to academics' analyses of government policy. Models, forecasts, and policy analysis are also key to understanding forecast uncertainty. Without public funding of forecast evaluation and of the modeling of structural change, policymakers would operate without the full set of tools that they require.

Acknowledgments

This research was partly financed by ESRC grants L116251012 "Macroeconomic Modeling: the United Kingdom and the World, 1995–1999" (with Martin Weale and Garry Young) and R02225166 "Do Small Differences Matter? The Structure and Consequence of Macroeconomic Differences between Members of EMU: January 1999–June 2000". Cooperation with Nigel Pain over the last eleven years has greatly increased the author's understanding of the world and how to model it. The author has also benefited greatly from cooperation with and the insights of Andy Blake and Garry Young for almost as long a period. More recently, Ian Hurst and Karen Dury have been excellent collaborators. Martin Weale has been an excellent Institute director for the period in which our understanding of forecast uncertainty has been consolidated into our research program. All of these individuals deserve credit for the work discussed herein.

10 The Costs of Forecast Errors

Terence Burns

Summary

This chapter discusses the costs associated with making errors in economic forecasts. After arguing the case for articulated econometric models, the empirical characteristics of forecast errors are analyzed. Forecast errors are largest when the most is happening in the economy. Forecast errors are correlated across variables, and they reflect external shocks—which were often not forecast—and inaccurate data about the recent past. This chapter then considers the implications of forecast errors, both within a given policy framework and for the choice of policy framework. Within a given policy framework, forecast errors may increase economic instability and hence affect longer-term economic performance. Forecast errors are also important to consider in the conduct of policy: better forecasts will allow economic gains, so the search for improved forecasting models and methods should continue.

10.1 Introduction

This chapter focuses on the costs associated with making errors in economic forecasts. Section 10.2 argues the case for producing detailed, coherent, and integrated forecasts of the economy; and it discusses various reasons why some people are suspicious about economic forecasts and their role in the policy process. Section 10.3 examines some characteristics of forecast errors. The discussion then turns to the costs of forecast errors, distinguishing between two situations in which forecasts can play an important role: one when implementing a given policy framework (Section 10.4), and the other when deciding to change the policy framework itself (Section 10.5).

This analysis draws on my years of involvement in economic forecasting, wearing many different hats. For 15 years at the London Business School (LBS) during the 1960s and 1970s, I participated in building forecasting models, making forecasts, and using both to offer published policy advice to the UK government. Indeed, Jim Ball presented the first version of the LBS model at a British Association meeting in Nottingham in 1966. Between 1980 and 1991, I was Chief Economic Adviser at Her Majesty's Treasury and so supervised the substantial UK Treasury forecasting team. While I was less involved in the details of forecasting by then, I still needed to be familiar with the forecasts, and I offered Ministers a commentary on the forecasts and my judgment of the policy implications. As Permanent Secretary to the UK Treasury from 1991 until 1998, I was substantially a customer of the forecasting process, although I retained a management role—particularly with regard to resources—and I continued to be involved in discussions about the policy implications of the forecasts.

10.2 The General Case for Economic Forecasting

Despite all the ups and downs of modeling, I remain persuaded of the general case for having a capacity to produce detailed, coherent, and integrated forecasts. I have often had to justify that case to government Ministers and others involved in the policy process: this section sets out the central arguments.

The economy is a complicated dynamic system subject to shocks and constant innovations and in which agents learn from experience. The economy involves long and complex lags, and changes in policy instruments can take substantial time to have an effect. Ideally, this means that policy interventions should be directed towards what is likely to happen some time in the future, rather than towards what happened yesterday.

Accumulating knowledge about this economic system is central to improving the conduct of policy. In particular, a detailed model of the economy—one that emphasizes the relationships between different parts of the economic system—helps in understanding that economic system itself. A detailed model also helps interpret past forecast errors, as through sorting out which links are weak or have broken down. Finally, when faced with new circumstances, a reasonably detailed model can be much more easily adapted to capture those circumstances than can "black-box" forecasting methods. See Chapters 3 and 9 for related arguments.

Despite these persuasive reasons for having a forecasting capacity based upon a reasonably detailed structural model of the economy, some participants in the policy debate are suspicious about forecasts and the role of forecasts in the policy process. The most important source of scepticism is the history of forecast errors. Forecast errors can be substantial on occasion, with periods of good forecast accuracy interrupted by periods of successive large errors. This chapter focuses on the implications of such errors.

There is also some concern that too much influence is in the hands of the forecasters, who impose their rigid and mechanical models of the economy on policy discussions. Critics worry that large models can be difficult to understand, and that their assumptions are often implicit rather than explicit, thereby making those models—if anything—more dangerous than alternative forecasting procedures. Large models can raise additional suspicion because it can be difficult to demonstrate the properties of—or to understand the main forces behind—a particular forecast. Likewise, it can be difficult to determine whether large models incorporate various widely believed, longer-term constraints of macroeconomic behavior, and hence whether those models have satisfactory longer-term properties.

Treasury Ministers also sometimes suspect that forecasts are deliberately cautious so as to satisfy the general Treasury desire for prudence and for keeping something in hand. I have often been called upon to satisfy Ministers that the forecast is the best available and not deliberately cautious. Forecasters are also criticized for paying too much attention to their models and not enough to what is actually happening in the economy. That said, I shall discuss later how the contribution of external information to the forecasting process is sometimes mixed.

All this said, the explicit and transparent nature of forecasting means that forecast errors are very evident and that they appear relatively quickly. Part of the value of forecasts is that they *are* transparent: they set out the detail for all to see, along with the assumptions. Forecasters sometimes complain that they can become scapegoats for policy mistakes and that their critics are selective in their own memories—which is only possible because those critics do not present their views with the same degree of transparency. Whatever the truth of this complaint, forecast errors will be made: it is in the nature of forecasting. Economic forecasting is rarely seen as a science. Instead, it is treated as some combination of an art-form and witchcraft—and a source of considerable suspicion, particularly during difficult periods.

10.3   Some Characteristics of Forecast Errors

The characteristics of forecast errors help in understanding the costs of forecast errors, so this section examines some of those characteristics. The corresponding sources of forecast errors are among those suggested by the theory in Chapter 11.

First, the largest forecast errors occur when the economy moves most sharply relative to its trend. While not surprising, this characteristic is a little disappointing because this is an instance in which users hope that forecasts could be most useful; see Chapter 1. Critics sometimes say that large errors tend to occur at turning points of the business cycle, just when accurate forecasts could be most useful. There is an issue of cause and effect, though: large fluctuations in the economy may owe something to large forecast errors. If the sharp movement in the economy had been foreseen, some offsetting action might have been possible.

Second, forecast errors tend to be correlated across variables. When the forecast of an important variable goes wrong, errors in forecasts of other variables tend to appear at the same time. For instance, large forecast errors for output tend to be accompanied by significant forecast errors for inflation. If output is stronger than expected, inflation tends to be lower than expected initially, followed by inflation being higher than expected about two years later. Booms tend to bring recessions in their wake because unexpectedly high inflation tends to lead

to a subsequent period of output weakness that is also not fully anticipated. Another striking example of this feature is the correlation between errors in forecasts of output and public finances. When output
is better than expected, public finances are also better than expected
because of increased tax collection and reduced spending on social se-
curity. Likewise, a subsequent (unexpected) recession brings a period
when public finances tend to deteriorate more than predicted. These
correlations are substantial. Inspection of past forecast errors suggests
that, for each percentage point that output is higher than expected, the
Public Sector Net Cash Requirement is nearly one percent of GDP better than expected.

Third, forecast errors often reflect difficulties in coping with external shocks. Such shocks come in two forms. In one, events have a much
bigger effect than expected. The most noticeable cases in postwar experience were probably the two oil-price shocks, with the second- and
third-round effects being much bigger than expected. In the contrasting case, the predicted effect does not occur, although policy has been
adjusted to deal with the fear that it might. One recent example is the
1987 stock market crash, when the expected effect on overall demand
did not materialize. The policy response to the East Asian crisis in 1997
and 1998 may be seen in a similar way.

Fourth, and relatedly, forecast errors may occur because policy re-
sponded to the forecast itself. For example, a forecast recession might
not happen because policy was adjusted to counter it. In my experience, this source of forecast error has not been a big problem; and in
principle it can be addressed in the diagnosis of forecast errors.

Fifth, forecast errors can arise because data about the recent past
are inaccurate. If the "initial conditions" for forecasting are wrong, it is
difficult to make accurate forecasts. Forecasters thus often find themselves forecasting the recent past as well as the future. Revisions to data
can change the picture substantially. To complicate matters further, I
suspect that large data revisions are more likely when the economy is
changing gear—precisely when forecast errors tend to be largest. Data
weaknesses add to the problems in forecasting.

Finally, from my interpretation of the research evidence as well as
from my own investigations, the profession appears to have made very
little progress in reducing the size of forecast errors over the past 30

years or so, whether for the United Kingdom, the United States, or other industrialized countries. This result is tentative because some periods are intrinsically more difficult to predict than others. It is also a surprise and a disappointment, considering the huge increases in computing capacity as well as the development of ideas in both economics and econometrics.

My personal explanation is that the world has become more complicated over time and that we have had to work hard just in order to "stand still". Several factors may be at work. First, the effects of a liberalized global financial system are much more difficult to predict than those of the previous system, which was generally based upon quantitative controls of credit and lending. Second, modeling the behavior of the growing service sector is more difficult than modeling the (declining) manufacturing sector, in part because of the relative difficulties of data measurement. Third, with a greater awareness and access to information, many of the players in the economy are seeking to base their behavior upon expectations of the conduct of government policy. That makes the behavior of the private sector even more difficult to model.

10.4   Forecast Errors Under a Given Policy Framework

In examining the costs of forecast errors, we should distinguish between the problems that forecast errors create when operating within a given policy framework, and the extent to which forecast errors influence the choice of policy framework. The first situation is ongoing and concerns the role that forecasts play in the successful implementation of policy: this is the "bread and butter" of the forecasting business. The second situation arises only occasionally because the framework for conducting policy itself typically changes only infrequently. When it does arise, we need to decide whether the policy framework should be changed and, if so, what should replace it. The current section discusses the first situation, while Section 10.5 discusses the second.

Consider the effect of forecast errors within a given policy framework—say, where the government has an objective for low or stable inflation. In a world with no long-term trade-off between inflation and output, the main cost of forecast errors is instability. Specifically, forecast errors are expected to lead to greater instability of output, inflation, and public finances. Such instability in turn might affect longer-term economic performance.

I should add a disclaimer for the benefit of forecasters themselves. While forecast errors *can* contribute to economic instability, instability can occur for other reasons as well. For example, the policy framework or the policy objectives may be inappropriate for the circumstances; or unpredicted, unpredictable external shocks may occur. Also, because forecasts are never used mechanically in the policy process, policy interventions themselves may or may not be based upon the forecasts.

Still, forecasts often do play a role in the policy process. Consider the present UK monetary policy framework based upon inflation targets, as discussed in Chapters 8 and 9. The Chancellor of the Exchequer has assigned the Bank of England the objective of hitting an inflation target of $2\frac{1}{2}\%$ per annum, and the Bank of England sets interest rates on a month-by-month basis so as to meet that objective. Analysis suggests that a change in interest rates has its maximum effect $1\frac{1}{2}$–2 years out. The first stage of the Bank's monthly control process thus involves forecasting the inflation rate over the next two years or so, assuming that interest rates remain unchanged. The second stage is to determine what path of interest rates will bring the forward profile of inflation on target. Sections 10.4.1 and 10.4.2 thus examine these two stages and their implications for forecast errors. As an illustration, Section 10.4.3 analyzes the costs of forecast errors for the UK's expansion and recession during the late 1980s and early 1990s. Section 10.4.4 characterizes the generic costs of forecast errors.

10.4.1 *A baseline forecast*

Three major issues should be considered when projecting inflation forward over the period that is necessary to exercise effective policy control. The first is the movement of output relative to its trend—what is sometimes called the "output gap". The second is the influence of world prices on UK inflation, with world prices themselves depending upon the output gap in the industrialized world. The third is the influence of the exchange rate. In each case, there is much uncertainty and so considerable scope for generating forecast errors.

The first factor—the *output gap*—has received greater prominence over the past decade or so. It has turned out to be a better way of formulating the implications of a vertical Phillips curve than the traditional unemployment rate. The central principle is that inflation tends to rise with a positive output gap and fall with a negative output gap. Thus, if inflation is above target, output will need to be (temporarily) below trend while inflation is brought back to the target. Once that has been achieved, output can continue to grow on trend. While this is a powerful framework for analysis, significant difficulties impede using these ideas in practice. For instance, output must be forecast over the relevant period, raising the issues mentioned earlier, including the problem of data revisions. The underlying trend in output also must be determined, and that trend appears to have changed significantly over time. The policymaker must keep up with such changes, but can only really identify them with any confidence after the event. When the trend changes, errors are more likely to be made.

The second major influence on domestic inflation is *world inflation*. On postwar data, UK inflation and world inflation are highly correlated and, if anything, UK behavior has tended to exaggerate what is happening elsewhere. In principle, world prices depend in part on the output gap for the world as a whole. This raises issues paralleling those with the domestic output gap: world output growth must be predicted, and the trend growth of world output assessed.

The third factor is the *exchange rate*. Although I have focused on the output gap and world prices, other factors such as the exchange rate can easily complicate this analysis. In fact, over the past 25 years, the exchange rate has been one of the biggest problems in forecasting. Whatever our ability to predict the behavior of real variables, I think that most forecasters would conclude that competitively determined asset prices—such as floating exchange rates—are much more difficult to predict.

The task facing the forecaster is, therefore, a considerable one. In addition to the many issues set out above, the forecast should account for a whole range of statistics—such as business surveys—that may confirm or throw suspicion on the model's forecasts. The correlation between some business survey series and economic activity has been impressive at times, particularly when external shocks have generated significant changes in business confidence. Forecasters therefore should seek a role for surveys within their forecasting apparatus, particularly for short-term prospects, where official data can be weak. However, incorporating survey data into a structural model is not easy: typically, forecasters simply examine discrepancies between their forecasts and the business surveys. That said, business surveys do not have a consistent record of adding to the accuracy of forecasts. For instance, UK business surveys published during Autumn 1998 and Winter 1998–1999 turned out to be too pessimistic, even when allowing for their focus on the manufacturing sector. Much judgment is thus necessary when using survey information to improve conventional forecasts.

10.4.2 *Forecasts under alternative interest-rate paths*

The previous subsection discussed some issues in forecasting inflation when an unchanged future interest rate is assumed. Once that forecast path has been prepared, we also need to determine what changes in the interest rate are necessary to deliver the inflation target. If anything, this latter process is even more hazardous than preparing the base forecast. Interest rates affect the economy through a multitude of channels, where the time lags can depend upon expectations, the circumstances of the time, and the nature of any "surprises". Key channels involve the exchange rate, the housing market, and inventories. Sustained changes in the interest rate may also affect consumer and investment spending.

Policy mistakes can arise from a poor baseline forecast, or from misjudging the change in interest rate necessary to deliver the objective for inflation. If mistakes are made, subsequent policy action may need to be more severe, and inflation may depart from target and output from its trend for a substantial period because of the lags within the economic system. As mentioned earlier, forecasting is more difficult when variables move sharply relative to trend. If a significant policy error takes the economy well away from its trend, the initial disturbance can persist for a long time. By analogy, the larger the stone thrown into the pond, the bigger the ripples and the longer they will be visible.

10.4.3 *An example of the costs of forecast errors*

The UK business cycle over the late 1980s and early 1990s highlights a large disturbance with very persistent effects; see both Chapters 4 and 7 for complementary perspectives. During 1987–1988, output grew much faster than expected and moved significantly above trend, and momentum carried the economy faster and farther than expected by forecasters. Simultaneously, house prices rose sharply, stimulated in part by the proposal in the budget to restrict mortgage interest tax relief to a single individual even when house purchase was shared. When the extent of the growth in demand was finally appreciated, a sharp increase in interest rates was necessary to deal with the resulting inflationary pressures. Inflation increased rapidly during 1988–1989, in part because mortgage costs (and hence interest rates) enter the UK's headline inflation rate.

Because of the government's concern about inflation, interest rates remained higher until inflation had clearly peaked. By that time, economic activity was falling, as were house prices. Declining house prices and growing indebtedness in turn created negative equity for some households, and the latter's effect on consumer spending was difficult to anticipate. The weakness in economic activity persisted longer than expected, and the level of output fell well below its trend. Inflation likewise fell further and faster than anticipated. Policy was eventually relaxed, output grew faster than trend for several years, and a balance was restored, with output close to trend and inflation in the range of 2%–4%. Since then, output has remained close to trend, inflation has been very stable, and forecast errors have been much smaller. The boom of 1987–1988 thus took some 6–7 years to play itself out, with a succession of forecasts that involved significant forecast errors for output, inflation, and public finances. Once calm was restored, the forecasting record improved.

The costs of that instability might well differ from those associated with a more benign scenario in which inflation had been gradually squeezed out of the economy, with a longer but less dramatic effect on the growth of output. I suspect that the differences in costs are significant, although the microeconomic aspects are easier to demonstrate than the macroeconomic ones.

10.4.4   *Generic costs of forecast errors*

This final subsection thus considers the generic costs of forecast errors. First, economic instability may affect the underlying growth rate of output, although I am unaware of any convincing evidence for such an effect in the United Kingdom. Such an effect is plausible, though, because instability does affect individual sectors and industries, and so their investment behavior. The goal of stabilizing output growth and inflation is based in part upon the view that doing so will improve the longer-term performance of the economy. The challenge is to assess that effect quantitatively and distinguish it from a host of other factors affecting the underlying growth rate. From looking at observed output, its trend rate of growth appears lower from the mid-1960s through the early 1970s than during the 1950s and early 1960s. Output growth appears to have slowed further after the oil-price crisis in 1973 and the resulting high inflation. Since the early 1980s, average growth has risen to about 2%–3%. The two oil-price hikes and the subsequent inflation appear to have been the biggest influences on the trend in output. These periods were also associated with economic instability generally, which complicates the analysis. The instability of the late 1980s and early 1990s may have affected the underlying growth rate, but there is no convincing evidence yet: subsequent experience may help.

Second, economic instability has microeconomic effects, which are clearly substantial. The effects of cyclical changes fall unevenly across the economy, with some industries and individuals hit much more severely than others. The housing market and related activities were particularly affected in the circumstances just described. Many individuals had taken on large mortgages and then suffered from both negative equity after house prices fell and escalating debt as repayments became difficult.

Third, economic instability can encumber other government policies. Achieving an appropriate balance between taxes and spending can be difficult in any circumstances, and public finances become an even more challenging task when economic activity is unstable. In fiscal policy, the biggest practical challenge is to distinguish the underlying economic performance from cyclical behavior and from the general noise affecting taxation and spending. The economic cycle affects both tax collection and public spending. Separating the underlying position from the cycle and general noise is crucial when deciding what changes are needed in the underlying position. The paradox is that, if monetary policy is successful and economic growth is reasonably steady, it is much easier to avoid mistakes in fiscal policy. That, in turn, adds further stability. Distinguishing the underlying movement from noise is much more difficult when the economy becomes volatile. The conduct of fiscal policy in turn becomes more difficult and often exacerbates the problem. In recent years—which contrast with the late 1980s and early 1990s—the government has found it easier to conduct fiscal policy because the cycle has been reasonably benign.

Fourth, instability can affect the credibility of the policy framework. Poor forecasts and economic instability inevitably raise questions about the policy framework in use, and how it permitted these events. Sometimes this lack of credibility might be good because it highlights the weaknesses of the policy process and can help bring about change. On other occasions, lack of credibility might lead to a premature move away from a useful policy framework. Without wishing to get into substance, I suspect that high inflation and high interest rates in the late 1980s played a part in the government's decision to join the Exchange Rate Mechanism (ERM). The unexpected length of the recession in the early 1990s and the continued unsuitability of German interest rates for UK circumstances were likewise crucial factors in the UK's exit from the ERM and the development of the subsequent policy framework of inflation targeting.

Fifth, instability can damage the credibility of the policymakers. Even if private-sector forecast errors are as large as official forecast errors, the former receive less attention than the latter. Private-sector forecast errors also generally are not taken into account when judging the performance of official forecasts. Ministers are well aware that incorrect forecasts can damage their reputations. It is no wonder that they often wish to distance themselves from forecasts; see Chapter 4.

Taken together, this is a formidable list of costs. I would not seek to argue that a successful economic policy requires accurate forecasts: the importance of forecasts in the operation of policy tends to be exaggerated. That said, improvements in forecasting can better the operation of a particular policy framework.

10.5 Choosing the Policy Framework

The costs of forecast errors may potentially influence the choice of policy framework. By their nature, decisions about the policy framework occur only infrequently. Over the past 25 years or so, there have been relatively few major shifts of policy framework in the United

Kingdom—just six in total. This section describes those shifts and discusses their implications for the costs of forecast errors.

The six major shifts in the UK's policy framework are as follows.

- *Monetary targeting.* The move in 1976 to monetary targets was as big a shift as any. It represented a move away from a targeting framework involving real variables to one focusing on nominal magnitudes. Initially, the main target variable was the broad measure of (nominal) money supply.
- *The Medium-term Financial Framework.* By early 1980, monetary targeting had evolved into the Medium-term Financial Framework, marking a further important step on this road. It included a fiscal framework to support the monetary framework, and a further development of a cash-based public expenditure control system.
- *A generalized nominal framework.* In the face of a sharp decline in inflation combined with the continuing rapid growth of broad money, the policy emphasis on broad money gradually diminished from 1981 onwards. The general notion of a nominal policy framework remained important, but policy moved to monitoring monetary conditions in a wider sense by tracking a variety of nominal magnitudes. After becoming the UK Chancellor of the Exchequer in 1983, Nigel Lawson conducted a substantial review of alternative policy frameworks, and broad money was officially dropped as the target in 1985.
- *Joining the ERM.* Joining the Exchange Rate Mechanism in 1990 was a big shift in policy. Policy remained in a nominal framework, but the objective became holding the exchange rate within a defined path relative to the Deutsche mark.
- *Exiting the ERM.* Exit from the Exchange Rate Mechanism in 1992 was involuntary. The subsequent move to inflation targeting sought to build on the pre-ERM policy, while at the same time accounting for some of that policy's perceived weaknesses.
- *Central bank independence.* In 1997, the Labour government granted operational independence to the Bank of England. This represented more of a switch in arrangements for delivering policy than a switch of policy, although the introduction of a symmetric target for inflation was important.

By their nature, such changes in the underlying policy framework are infrequent. Forecasts do not typically play a decisive part in that choice, which focuses on a wider range of considerations. However, policy switches often do follow a period of difficulty with the previous policy regime, usually including significant forecast errors, so confidence in the forecasting process is not usually high when designing the new framework.

That said, the forecasting machinery can help analyze alternative frameworks, particularly when assessing where strains are likely to be felt. Such an assessment might examine the prospects for economic activity, inflation, etc. under different frameworks. In general, this assessment focuses less on point forecasts and more on the economy's likely response to shocks, the role of the implicit feedback systems, and the economy's robustness to surprises. The forecasting machinery also can aid operational decisions that have to be made when introducing a new framework, as with the quantification of targets.

In some instances, the chosen form of a policy framework might not have been adopted, had it been possible to predict events over the following two or three years. For example, the debate over joining the ERM might have proceeded differently if the subsequent problem with the housing market and the continued high level of German interest rates had been forecast. However, in general, the success of the design of a policy framework probably does not owe a great deal to forecasts; and forecast errors are usually not an important factor in choosing the framework.

Forecasts and forecast errors do matter insofar as they contribute to making a success of policy innovations. In the initial—and hence very uncertain—period of a new policy framework, forecast errors can matter because the short-run success of a policy change helps its longer-term credibility. For example, the perceived success of the new arrangements for monetary policy over 1997–1999 significantly affected the credibility of the process and tilted the balance of views about the design of the policy.

10.6 Conclusions

To summarize, I have argued the general case for a forecasting capacity that utilizes the available data as efficiently as possible. At the same time, it is important to recognize some of the disappointments with the forecast record that emerge from time to time. While forecast accuracy has not improved as much as might have been hoped for, given the dramatic improvements in computing, the increased complexities in the world economy may be responsible.

Forecast errors are important to consider in the conduct of policy. The most important cost of forecast errors arises from their contribution to the instability of output, inflation, and public finances. That instability can generate follow-on effects for some time and can have important effects on specific individuals and industries. Economic instability encumbers other government policies, particularly fiscal policy; and it can affect the credibility of the policy framework and of the policymakers. Better forecasts can lead to gains in the conduct of policy, so we should continue to search for improvements in forecasting.

11   Epilogue

David F. Hendry and Neil R. Ericsson

Summary

This epilogue places the book's chapters in a unified perspective, drawing on additional recent results from the literature on economic forecasting. We begin with a general retrospective (Section 11.1) that examines what can be proved about economic forecasts under two widely used sets of assumptions about forecasting models. The first set of assumptions asserts that the models are "good" representations of the economy over the forecast period. One can then prove that, on average, the "best" model produces the best forecasts, and that forecast errors will lie inside their confidence intervals the anticipated percentage of the time. Unfortunately, such outcomes are not realized in practice. We thus examine a second set of assumptions, in which models may poorly characterize complicated and possibly rapidly changing economies. These assumptions give rise to a different set of theorems, which suggest that "robust" forecasting models—those that adjust rapidly to unanticipated large shocks—will do best in many settings.

Finally, we indicate how a taxonomy for the sources of forecast errors leads to a more formal approach for analyzing economic forecasts (Section 11.2). This approach permits evaluating the sources that might precipitate systematic forecast failure, and so it can help design and select forecasting techniques that would mitigate such problems.

11.1   A Retrospective

We hope that the reader has now acquired a better understanding of economic forecasts. This book has addressed what forecasts are, who constructs and who uses forecasts, how forecasting is done, how the success or failure of forecasts is measured, what the costs of forecast errors comprise, what forecast uncertainty is, how it is measured, and what degree of confidence should be placed in economic forecasts. This book also discussed the construction of econometric models, the properties of forecasting methods, the main problems in economic forecasting, and some possible solutions. Forecasting practices at the Bank of England, Her Majesty's Treasury, and NIESR *inter alia* illustrated the issues that arose. The remainder of this section reiterates and synthesizes these central themes.

At first sight, an economic forecast seems like a straightforward entity—it is a statement about the likely future outcome of an economic variable, e.g., of inflation. Underlying such forecasts are many layers, which this book has sought to delineate. There are numerous ways of generating economic forecasts. Many are a mix of science—based on rigorously tested econometric systems—and judgment, occasioned by unexpected events: the future is not always like the present or the past.

Historically, the theory of forecasting that underpinned actual practice in economics has relied on two key assumptions—that the model was a good representation of the economy, and that the structure of the economy would remain relatively unchanged. Under these assumptions, several important theorems can be proved. First, the "best" model generally produces the best forecasts, so it doesn't pay to use an average of forecasts across several models; see Clements and Hendry (1998, 1999) for details and proofs. Second, forecast accuracy declines as the forecast horizon increases. Third, the calculated confidence interval around a forecast provides a good guide to the likely variation in the forecast error.

Empirical experience in economic forecasting has highlighted the poverty of the two traditional assumptions. Many econometric models for forecasting are known to be seriously mis-specified, and the actual economy has been subject to important but unanticipated shifts, so forecast failure has been a relatively common phenomenon. Also, the implications of the above theory are inconsistent with the results of empirical forecasting competitions between many models on numerous time series. Simple methods often outperform better-fitting ones, and pooling of forecasts (i.e., using an average of forecasts) can pay: Makridakis and Hibon (2000) record the latest in a sequence of such findings. Furthermore, which model does "best" in a forecasting competition depends upon how the forecasts are evaluated, as discussed at length in Chapters 2, 4, 5, and 6.

Recent forecast theory makes less stringent assumptions: the model may be a greatly simplified representation that is incorrect in many respects, and the economy may both evolve and suddenly shift. After any sudden and unexpected shift, the forecasts from a pre-existing model are unlikely to match the outcomes closely. In this more realistic setting, none of the theorems noted above hold: the best model in-sample need not produce the best forecasts; pooling of forecasts may pay; longer-term forecasts may be more accurate than short-term ones; and calculated confidence intervals can be seriously misleading about actual forecast uncertainty.

More fundamentally, causal variables (a shorthand for the variables that actually determine the outcome) need not help a model's forecasts either. Following a shift in the economy, a previously well-specified model can forecast less accurately than a model in which none of its right-hand side variables are relevant in the underlying relationship. While shocking at first blush, this result helps account for the rankings in published forecasting competitions. The model providing the best description of the economy may not be as robust to sudden shifts as a simpler and more adaptive model, so the former model may lose to the latter in forecasting over periods when shifts occurred. Also, pooling can be beneficial because different models are differentially affected by unanticipated shifts. Finally, because the effects of a levels shift may wear off on data transformations such as growth rates, longer-term forecasts can be more accurate than even one-step ahead forecasts made a few periods after a shift. The shift can temporarily contaminate a model's short-term forecasts.

Forecast uncertainty is central to understanding economic forecasts themselves. Several chapters emphasized the difference between the uncertainties of which modelers are aware and the uncertainty arising from those "things we don't know we don't know". Chapters 1, 2, and 5 discussed implications of that distinction at a theoretical level; and Chapters 2, 4, 8, and 9 considered how that distinction could be handled in practice. While the unpredictable cannot be forecast, early warning devices can be developed as harbingers of impending problems, and rare events may prove partly predictable. Even rare events have causes, and some of those causes may be discernible in advance, as shown in Chapter 7. Nevertheless, perfect forecasts are not in the offing. A realistic alternative is to construct forecasts that adapt quickly after any mistake is discovered, so that systematic forecast failure does not ensue. Thus, econometric models might be redesigned to capture some of the robustness of the simple models that win forecasting competitions. To indicate how such redesign might proceed, the next section categorizes the sources of forecast errors and examines the relative importance of those sources.

11.2 A More Formal Approach

Clements and Hendry (1999, Chapter 2) propose a taxonomy for all sources of forecast errors. That taxonomy underpins a more formal theory of forecasting, which Clements and Hendry develop. This section summarizes that taxonomy and highlights some of its implications.

Econometric models typically have deterministic terms such as intercepts and trends, stochastic terms such as inflation and output, and unobserved errors or shocks. Clements and Hendry (1999) thus delineate the following nine sources of forecast error:

  (1) shifts in the coefficients on deterministic terms,
  (2) shifts in the coefficients on stochastic terms,
  (3) mis-specification of deterministic terms,
  (4) mis-specification of stochastic terms,
  (5) mis-estimation of the coefficients on deterministic terms,
  (6) mis-estimation of the coefficients on stochastic terms,
  (7) mis-measurement of the data,
  (8) changes in the variances of the errors, and
  (9) errors cumulating over the forecast horizon.

Each of these nine sources could induce substantial forecast errors. However, detailed theoretical analyses, computer-based Monte Carlo simulations, and empirical evidence all suggest that Source #1 is the most pernicious. Shifts in the coefficients on deterministic terms are equivalent to shifts in the deterministic terms themselves, so that is how Clements and Hendry interpret that source. Such shifts typically induce large and systematic forecast failure, whereas the other sources of forecast error have less damaging effects. For example, even quite large shifts in a model's coefficients on stochastic variables (Source #2)—such as α_2 in Chapter 3's equation (3.3)—have little effect on forecast errors, provided no deterministic shifts occur; see Hendry (2000) *inter alia*. Similar comments apply to Sources ##3–6; see Clements and Hendry (1999). As Chapter 10 notes, data inaccuracy at the forecast's origin (Source #7) can deleteriously affect forecasts because the measurement error acts like a deterministic shift. Likewise, any sufficiently large stochastic perturbation (Sources #8 and #9) will reduce forecast accuracy; but, in general, Source #1 is the culprit when forecast failure occurs.

Some interesting implications follow. First, model forms that inherently preclude deterministic terms can never suffer deterministic shifts, and so are unlikely to experience systematic forecast failure. This is consistent with the findings in Eitrheim, Husebø and Nymoen (1999), who compare some forecasting devices that should be immune to Source #1 with the Norges Bank econometric model, which can suffer from deterministic shifts. Eitrheim *et al.* (1999) find that "robust" forecast devices usually outperform the Norges Bank model over the short term (up to a year ahead), particularly over periods where the Bank's model did badly. However, the Norges Bank model does best over longer horizons (3 years ahead) when the greater forecast-error variances of the simpler devices offset their smaller biases. These findings are in line with the theoretical predictions of recent forecast theory.

Second, reformulating econometric models to make them more robust to such shifts becomes a priority. Current best practice in econometrics uses the technique of cointegration to remove another form of non-stationarity, that due to stochastic trends or unit roots; see Hendry and Juselius (2000, 2001) for recent expositions. Chapters 3 and 9 in particular stressed the importance of models having coherent long-run properties; cointegration is a widely used approach for imposing such equilibrium relations. Unfortunately, cointegration makes the resulting models sensitive to shifts in the equilibrium mean.

Third, a potential solution is intercept correction, which is the practice of adjusting an equation's constant term when forecasting. Historically, intercept correction has been heavily criticized, as witnessed by some of its alternative, emotive names: con factor, cheat term, and *ad hoc* adjustment. In intercept correction, the model is placed back on track at the forecast origin: the most recent *ex post* forecast error is set to zero. That procedure offsets deterministic shifts after they have occurred; and it should almost always be implemented if shifts are suspected, as they would be if forecast failure recently occurred. Intercept correction thus can mitigate a model's sensitivity to shifts, where that sensitivity was induced by incorporating equilibrium relations through cointegration analysis.

The key insight into why intercept corrections might be useful arises from the earlier, apparently worrying result that models with no causal variables might outperform those with numerous correctly included causal variables. Intercept corrections reflect and so offset the deterministic shifts that can swamp useful information from causal factors. Intercept corrections have long been known to improve forecast performance in practice: see Turner (1990) *inter alia*. Thus, far from being a pessimistic result, the refutation of the claim that causal models will outperform non-causal models is an important step towards understanding the actual behavior of economic forecasts. That insight—combined with explanations for the results of forecasting competitions and for the relative performance of short-term and longer-run forecasts—suggests that a sustainable framework for interpreting forecasts is emerging.

11.3   Concluding Remarks

Economists have developed new extensive theories of economic forecasting under relatively realistic assumptions, and they have begun testing the implications of those theories in practical settings. We have reviewed some of the many intriguing implications from these recent developments. For example, we now understand the sources of forecast failure and can explain the rankings of models in forecasting competitions. As Section 11.1 discussed, earlier forecasting theorems are unreliable in practice. In particular, contrary to one of those earlier theorems, causal variables need not improve forecasts. New theorems are now replacing those older theorems, and the new ones are more consonant with the historical performance of economic forecasts.

The reader may wonder why economists persist in developing econometric models that seek to elucidate the causal connections in an economy if such models cannot be shown to be of value in forecasting. The answer comes in two parts. First, models are needed to address policy issues, and no current theorems justify non-causal models in the policy domain. Second, the characteristics of "robustness" and "rapid adaptation" to breaks have determined the winners of economic forecasting competitions. Such characteristics can be transferred to econometric models, albeit in modified ways, without impugning the value of those econometric models in policy analyses: see Hendry and Mizon (2000). While much analysis remains to establish the most appropriate forecast procedures, these recent advances support an optimism about the future of economic forecasting.

References

Acemoglu, D. and Scott, A. (1994). Asymmetries in the cyclical behaviour of UK labour markets. *Economic Journal*, **104**, 1303–1323.

Allsopp, C., Jenkinson, T. and Morris, D. (1991). The assessment: Macroeconomic policy in the 1980s. *Oxford Review of Economic Policy*, **7**, 68–80.

Anderton, R. and Barrell, R. (1995). The ERM and structural change in European labour markets: A study of 10 countries. *Weltwirtschaftliches Archiv*, **131**, 47–66.

Andrews, D. W. K. (1993). Tests for parameter instability and structural change with unknown change point. *Econometrica*, *61*(4), 821–856.

Baba, Y., Hendry, D. F. and Starr, R. M. (1992). The demand for M1 in the U.S.A., 1960–1988. *Review of Economic Studies*, *59*(1), 25–61.

Bank of England (1999). *Economic Models at the Bank of England*. London: Bank of England.

Bank of England (2000). *Inflation Report: November 2000*. London: Bank of England.

Bank of Thailand (2000). *Inflation Report: July 2000*. Bangkok: Bank of Thailand.

Barrell, R. (ed.) (1994). *The UK Labour Market*. Cambridge: Cambridge University Press.

Barrell, R., Anderton, R., Lansbury, M. L. and Sefton, J. (1998). FEERs for the NIEs. In Collignon, S., Park, Y. C. and Pisani-Ferry, J. (eds.) , *Exchange Rate Policies in Emerging Asian Countries*, pp. 245–279. London: Routledge.

Barrell, R. and Dury, K. (2001). Asymmetric labour markets in a converging Europe. Working paper no. 2, ENEPRI, Brussels.

Barrell, R., Dury, K., Holland, D., Pain, N. and te Velde, D. (1998). Financial market contagion and the effects of the crises in East Asia, Russia and Latin America. *National Institute Economic Review*, **166**, 57–73.

Barrell, R., Dury, K. and Hurst, I. (2001). Forecasting in an uncertain world. Mimeo, National Institute, London.

Barrell, R. and Genre, V. (1999). Employment strategies for Europe: Lessons from Denmark and the Netherlands. *National Institute Economic Review*, **168**, 82–98.

Barrell, R. and Morgan, J. (1996). International comparisons of labour market responses to economic recovery. Report rs 38, Department for Education and Employment (DfEE), London.

Barrell, R. and Pain, N. (1998). Developments in East Asia and their implications for the UK and Europe. *National Institute Economic Review*, **163**, 64–70.

Batini, N. and Haldane, A. G. (1999a). Forward-looking rules for monetary policy. Working paper, 91, Bank of England, London.

Batini, N. and Haldane, A. G. (1999b). Monetary policy rules and inflation forecasts. *Bank of England Quarterly Bulletin*, **39**, 60–67.

Bean, C. R. (1998). The new UK monetary arrangements: A view from the literature. *Economic Journal*, **108**, 1795–1809.

Birchenhall, C. R., Jessen, H., Osborn, D. R. and Simpson, P. W. (1999). Predicting US business-cycle regimes. *Journal of Business and Economic Statistics*, **17**, 313–323.

Birchenhall, C. R., Osborn, D. R. and Sensier, M. (2001). Predicting UK business cycle regimes. *Scottish Journal of Political Economy*, **48**, 179–195.

Blake, A. (2000). Optimality and Taylor rules. *National Institute Economic Review*, **174**, 80–91.

Box, G. E. P. and Jenkins, G. M. (1970). *Time Series Analysis: Forecasting and Control*. San Francisco: Holden-Day.

Britton, E., Fisher, P. and Whitley, J. (1998). *Inflation Report* projections: Understanding the fan chart. *Bank of England Quarterly Bulletin*, **38**, 30–37.

Budd, A. (1998). Economic policy, with and without forecasts. *Bank of England Quarterly Bulletin*, **38**, 379–384.

Burns, T. (1986). The interpretation and use of economic predictions. *Proceedings of the Royal Society*, **A407**, 103–125.

Calvo, G. A. (1983). Staggered prices in a utility-maximizing framework. *Journal of Monetary Economics*, **12**, 383–398.

Campos, J. (1992). Confidence intervals for linear combinations of forecasts from dynamic econometric models. *Journal of Policy Modeling*, *14*(4), 535–560.

Central Statistical Office (1993). *Economic Trends Annual Supplement*. London: H.M.S.O.

Chong, Y. Y. and Hendry, D. F. (1986). Econometric evaluation of linear macro-economic models. *Review of Economic Studies*, *53*(4), 671–690.

Chow, G. C. (1960). Tests of equality between sets of coefficients in two linear regressions. *Econometrica*, **28**, 591–605.

Clements, M. P. and Hendry, D. F. (1993). On the limitations of comparing mean square forecast errors. *Journal of Forecasting*, *12*(8), 617–637. With discussion and reply.

Clements, M. P. and Hendry, D. F. (1998). *Forecasting Economic Time Series*. Cambridge: Cambridge University Press.

Clements, M. P. and Hendry, D. F. (1999). *Forecasting Non-stationary Economic Time Series*. Cambridge, Mass.: MIT Press.

Clements, M. P. and Hendry, D. F. (2000). Forecasting with difference-stationary and trend-stationary models. *Econometrics Journal*, *4*(1), S1–S19.

Clements, M. P. and Hendry, D. F. (eds.) (2001a). *Companion to Economic Forecasting*. Oxford: Blackwell Publishers. Forthcoming.

Clements, M. P. and Hendry, D. F. (2001b). An historical perspective on forecast errors. *National Institute Economic Review*, **177**, 100–112.

Clements, M. P. and Krolzig, H.-M. (1998). A comparison of the forecast performance of Markov-switching and threshold autoregressive models of US GNP. *Econometrics Journal*, **1**, C47–C75.

Clements, M. P. and Smith, J. (1999). A Monte Carlo study of the forecasting performance of empirical SETAR models. *Journal of Applied Econometrics*, **14**, 124–141.

Cook, S. (1995). Treasury economic forecasting. Mimeo, Institute of Economics and Statistics, University of Oxford.

Crafts, N. F. R. and Harley, C. K. (1992). Output growth and the British Industrial Revolution: A restatement of the Crafts–Harley view. *Economic History Review*, **45**, 703–730.

Diebold, F. X. (1998). The past, present and future of macroeconomic forecasting. *Journal of Economic Perspectives*, **12**, 175–192.

Diebold, F. X. and Chen, C. (1996). Testing structural stability with endogenous breakpoint: A size comparison of analytic and bootstrap procedures. *Journal of Econometrics*, **70**, 221–241.

Doornik, J. A. and Hendry, D. F. (1996). *PcGive Professional 9.0 for Windows*. London: International Thomson Business Press.

Doornik, J. A. and Hendry, D. F. (2001a). *GiveWin: An Interface to Empirical Modelling*. London: Timberlake Consultants Press.

Doornik, J. A. and Hendry, D. F. (2001b). *Modelling Dynamic Systems using PcGive 10: Volume II*. London: Timberlake Consultants Press.

Doornik, J. A., Hendry, D. F. and Nielsen, B. (1998). Inference in cointegrated models: UK M1 revisited. *Journal of Economic Surveys*, **12**, 533–572.

Dornbusch, R. (1976). Expectations and exchange rate dynamics. *Journal of Political Economy*, **84**, 1161–1176.

Dow, C. (1998). *Major Recessions: Britain and the World, 1920–1995*. Oxford: Oxford University Press.

Durbin, J. and Watson, G. S. (1950). Testing for serial correlation in least squares regression I. *Biometrika*, **37**, 409–428.

Durbin, J. and Watson, G. S. (1951). Testing for serial correlation in least squares regression II. *Biometrika*, **38**, 159–178.

Eitrheim, Ø., Husebø, T. A. and Nymoen, R. (1999). Equilibrium-correction versus differencing in macroeconometric forecasting. *Economic Modelling*, **16**, 515–544.

Engle, R. F. (1982). Autoregressive conditional heteroscedasticity, with estimates of the variance of United Kingdom inflation. *Econometrica*, **50**, 987–1007.

Engle, R. F. and Hendry, D. F. (1993). Testing super exogeneity and invariance in regression models. *Journal of Econometrics*, **56**, 119–139.

Ericsson, N. R. (1992). Parameter constancy, mean square forecast errors, and measuring forecast performance: An exposition, extensions, and illustration. *Journal of Policy Modeling*, 14(4), 465–495.

Ericsson, N. R. (2001). Forecast uncertainty in economic modeling. International finance discussion paper no. 697, Board of Governors of the Federal Reserve System, Washington, D.C.

Ericsson, N. R., Campos, J. and Tran, H.-A. (1990). PC-GIVE and David Hendry's econometric methodology. *Revista de Econometria*, **10**, 7–117.

Ericsson, N. R., Hendry, D. F. and Prestwich, K. M. (1998). The demand for broad money in the United Kingdom, 1878–1993. *Scandinavian Journal of Economics*, 100(1), 289–324. With discussion.

Ericsson, N. R. and Irons, J. S. (1995). The Lucas critique in practice: Theory without measurement. In Hoover, K. D. (ed.), *Macroeconometrics: Developments, Tensions, and Prospects*, Ch. 8, pp. 263–312. Boston, Massachusetts: Kluwer Academic Publishers. With discussion.

Ericsson, N. R. and Marquez, J. (1993). Encompassing the forecasts of U.S. trade balance models. *Review of Economics and Statistics*, 75(1), 19–31.

Ericsson, N. R. and Marquez, J. (1998). A framework for economic forecasting. *Econometrics Journal*, 1(1), C228–C266.

Filardo, A. J. (1994). Business–cycle phases and their transitional dynamics. *Journal of Business and Economic Statistics*, **12**, 299–308.

Franz, W. and Steiner, V. (2000). Wages in the East German transition process: Facts and explanations. *German Economic Review*, **1**, 241–270.

Friedman, M. (1960). *A Program for Monetary Stability*. New York: Fordham University Press.

Godfrey, L. G. (1978). Testing for higher order serial correlation in regression equations when the regressors include lagged dependent variables. *Econometrica*, **46**, 1303–1313.

Goldfeld, S. M. (1973). The demand for money revisited. *Brookings Papers on Economic Activity*, 1973(3), 577–638. With discussion.

Goldfeld, S. M. (1976). The case of the missing money. *Brookings Papers on Economic Activity*, 1976(3), 683–730. With discussion.

Gould, S. J. (2000). *The Lying Stones of Marrakech.* Random House, London: Johanthan Cape.

Granger, C. W. J. (1999). *Empirical Modeling in Economics: Specification and Evaluation.* Cambridge: Cambridge University Press.

Granger, C. W. J. and Pesaran, M. H. (2000a). A decision-theoretic approach to forecast evaluation. In Chon, W. S., Li, W. K. and Tong, H. (eds.) , *Statistics and Finance: An Interface*, pp. 261–278. London: Imperial College Press.

Granger, C. W. J. and Pesaran, M. H. (2000b). Economic and statistical measures of forecasting accuracy. *Journal of Forecasting*, **19**, 537–560.

Granger, C. W. J. and Teräsvirta, T. (1993). *Modelling Nonlinear Economic Relationships.* Oxford: Oxford University Press.

Hamilton, J. D. (1989). A new approach to the economic analysis of nonstationary time series and the business cycle. *Econometrica*, **57**, 357–384.

Hansen, B. E. (1992a). Testing for parameter instability in linear models. *Journal of Policy Modeling*, **14**(4), 517–533.

Hansen, B. E. (1992b). Tests for parameter instability in regressions with I(1) processes. *Journal of Business and Economic Statistics*, **10**(3), 321–335.

Hendry, D. F. (1979). Predictive failure and econometric modelling in macroeconomics: The transactions demand for money. In Ormerod, P. (ed.) , *Economic Modelling*, pp. 217–242. London: Heinemann. Reprinted in Hendry, D. F., *Econometrics: Alchemy or Science?* Oxford: Blackwell Publishers, 1993, and Oxford University Press, 2000.

Hendry, D. F. (1987). Econometric methodology: A personal perspective. In Bewley, T. F. (ed.) , *Advances in Econometrics: Fifth World Congress*, Vol. 2, Ch. 10, pp. 29–48. Cambridge: Cambridge University Press.

Hendry, D. F. (1988). The encompassing implications of feedback versus feedforward mechanisms in econometrics. *Oxford Economic Papers*, **40**(1), 132–149.

Hendry, D. F. (1995). *Dynamic Econometrics.* Oxford: Oxford University Press.

Hendry, D. F. (2000). On detectable and non-detectable structural change. *Structural Change and Economic Dynamics*, **11**, 45–65.

Hendry, D. F. and Doornik, J. A. (1994). Modelling linear dynamic econometric systems. *Scottish Journal of Political Economy*, **41**, 1–33.

Hendry, D. F. and Doornik, J. A. (2001). *Empirical Econometric Modelling using PcGive 10: Volume I.* London: Timberlake Consultants Press.

Hendry, D. F. and Ericsson, N. R. (1991). Modeling the demand for narrow money in the United Kingdom and the United States. *European Economic Review*, **35**, 833–886.

Hendry, D. F. and Juselius, K. (2000). Explaining cointegration analysis: Part I. *Energy Journal*, **21**, 1–42.

Hendry, D. F. and Juselius, K. (2001). Explaining cointegration analysis: Part II. *Energy Journal*, **22**, 75–120.

Hendry, D. F. and Mizon, G. E. (1993). Evaluating dynamic econometric models by encompassing the VAR. In Phillips, P. C. B. (ed.) , *Models, Methods and Applications of Econometrics*, pp. 272–300. Oxford: Basil Blackwell.

Hendry, D. F. and Mizon, G. E. (2000). Reformulating empirical macroeconometric modelling. *Oxford Review of Economic Policy*, **16**, 138–159.

Hendry, D. F., Pagan, A. and Sargan, J. D. (1984). Dynamic specification. In Griliches, Z. and Intriligator, M. D. (eds.) , *Handbook of Econometrics*, Vol. 2, Ch. 18, pp. 1023–1100. Amsterdam: North-Holland.

Hoover, K. D. and Perez, S. J. (1999). Data mining reconsidered: Encompassing and the general-to-specific approach to specification search. *Econometrics Journal*, 2(2), 167–191. With discussion.

Jarque, C. M. and Bera, A. K. (1980). Efficient tests for normality, homoscedasticity and serial independence of regression residuals. *Economics Letters*, **6**, 255–259.

Johansen, S. (1992). Testing weak exogeneity and the order of cointegration in UK money demand. *Journal of Policy Modeling*, **14**, 313–334.

Judd, J. P. and Scadding, J. L. (1982). The search for a stable money demand function: A survey of the post-1973 literature. *Journal of Economic Literature*, 20(3), 993–1023.

Kiviet, J. F. (1986). On the rigour of some mis-specification tests for modelling dynamic relationships. *Review of Economic Studies*, **53**, 241–261.

Krolzig, H.-M. and Hendry, D. F. (2001). Computer automation of general-to-specific model selection procedures. *Journal of Economic Dynamics and Control*, 25(6–7), 831–866.

Krolzig, H.-M. and Sensier, M. (2000). A disaggregated Markov–switching model of the UK business cycle. *Manchester School*, **68**, 442–460.

Lucas, Jr., R. E. (1976). Econometric policy evaluation: A critique. In Brunner, K. and Meltzer, A. (eds.) , *The Phillips Curve and Labor Markets*, Vol. 1 of *Carnegie-Rochester Conferences on Public Policy*, pp. 19–46. Amsterdam: North-Holland Publishing Company.

Makridakis, S. and Hibon, M. (2000). The M3-competition: Results, conclusions and implications. *International Journal of Forecasting*, **16**, 451–476.

Marget, A. W. (1929). Morgenstern on the methodology of economic forecasting. *Journal of Political Economy*, **37**, 312–339.

Marquez, J. and Ericsson, N. R. (1993). Evaluating forecasts of the U.S. trade balance. In Bryant, R. C., Hooper, P. and Mann, C. L. (eds.) , *Evaluating Policy Regimes: New Research in Empirical Macroeconomics*, Ch. 14, pp. 671–732. Washington, D.C.: Brookings Institution.

Mills, T. C. (1995). Are there asymmetries or nonlinearities in UK output?. *Applied Economics*, **27**, 1211–1217.

Mitchell, B. R. (1988). *British Historical Statistics*. Cambridge: Cambridge University Press.

Monetary Policy Committee (1999). The transmission mechanism of monetary policy. Report, Bank of England, London.

Morgan, J. (1996a). Structural change in European labour markets. *National Institute Economic Review*, **155**, 81–84.

Morgan, J. (1996b). What do comparisons of the last two economic recoveries tell us about the UK labour market. *National Institute Economic Review*, **156**, 80–92.

Morgenstern, O. (1928). *Wirtschaftsprognose: eine Untersuchung ihrer Voraussetzungen und Möglichkeiten*. Vienna: Julius Springer.

NIESR (1999). National Institute world model. Html, National Institute, London.

Öcal, N. and Osborn, D. R. (2000). Business cycle non-linearities in UK consumption and production. *Journal of Applied Econometrics*, **15**, 27–43.

Pain, N. and Britton, A. (1992). National Institute economic forecasts 1968 to 1991: Some tests of forecast properties. *National Institute Economic Review*, **141**, 81–93.

Paroulo, P. (1996). On the determination of integration indices in I(2) systems. *Journal of Econometrics*, **72**, 313–356.

Pesaran, M. H. and Potter, S. M. (1997). A floor and ceiling model of US Output. *Journal of Economic Dynamics and Control*, **21**, 661–695.

Rahbek, A., Kongsted, H. C. and Jørgensen, C. (1999). Trend-stationarity in the I(2) cointegration model. *Journal of Econometrics*, **90**, 265–289.

Simpson, P. W., Osborn, D. R. and Sensier, M. (2001). Modelling business cycle movements in the UK economy. *Economica*, **68**, 243–267.

Singer, M. (1997). Thoughts of a nonmillenarian. *Bulletin of the American Academy of Arts and Sciences*, **51**(2), 36–51.

Taylor, J. B. (1979). Staggered wage setting in a macro model. *American Economic Review*, **69**, 108–113.

Taylor, J. B. (1993). Discretion versus rules in practice. *Carnegie Rochester Series on Public Policy*, **39**, 195–214.

Teräsvirta, T. and Anderson, H. M. (1992). Characterizing nonlinearities in business cycles using smooth transition autoregressive models. *Journal of Applied Econometrics*, **7**, 119–139.

Turner, D. S. (1990). The role of judgement in macroeconomic forecasting. *Journal of Forecasting*, **9**, 315–345.

Vickers, J. (1999). Economic models and monetary policy. *Bank of England Quarterly Bulletin*, **39**, 210–216.

Wallis, K. F. (1989). Macroeconomic forecasting: A survey. *Economic Journal*, **99**, 28–61.

Wallis, K. F. (1999). Asymmetric density forecasts of inflation and the Bank of England's fan chart. *National Institute Economic Review*, **167**, 106–112.

Wallis, K. F. (2000). Macroeconometric modelling. In Gudmundsson, M., Herbertsson, T. T. and Zoega, G. (eds.) , *Macroeconomic Policy: Iceland in an Era of Global Integration*, pp. 399–414. Reykjavik: University of Iceland Press.

West, K. D. (1996). Asymptotic inference about predictive ability. *Econometrica,* **64**, 1067–1084.

Author Index

Acemoglu, D.   107, 113
Allsopp, C.   105, 107
Anderson, H. M.   112
Anderton, R.   152, 154
Andrews, D. W. K.   89

Baba, Y.   89
Bank of England   71, 72, 124, 145
Bank of Thailand   73
Barrell, R.   152, 154, 156, 159, 164, 165
Batini, N.   48
Bean, C. R.   48
Bera, A. K.   45
Birchenhall, C. R.   106, 109, 122, 123
Blake, A.   166
Box, G. E. P.   76
Britton, A.   24
Britton, E.   132
Budd, A.   126
Burns, T.   24

Calvo, G. A.   48, 50
Campos, J.   29, 89
Central Statistical Office   35
Chen, C.   113
Chong, Y. Y.   89
Chow, G. C.   89
Clements, M. P.   2, 7, 21, 24, 69, 76, 78, 113, 121, 153, 164, 186, 188, 189
Cook, S.   24
Crafts, N. F. R.   35

Diebold, F. X.   23, 113
Doornik, J. A.   29, 41, 74, 75, 92, 123
Dornbusch, R.   48
Dow, C.   106, 107, 116
Durbin, J.   45

Dury, K.   154, 159, 164, 165

Eitrheim, Ø.   189
Engle, R. F.   45, 89
Ericsson, N. R.   29, 69, 70, 79, 87, 89, 92

Filardo, A. J.   113, 116
Fisher, P.   132
Franz, W.   154
Friedman, M.   49

Genre, V.   156
Godfrey, L. G.   45
Goldfeld, S. M.   89
Gould, S. J.   29
Granger, C. W. J.   100, 101, 103, 112

Haldane, A. G.   48
Hamilton, J. D.   112
Hansen, B. E.   89
Harley, C. K.   35
Hendry, D. F.   2, 7, 21, 24, 29, 41, 69, 74–76, 78, 79, 86, 89, 92, 123, 153, 164, 186, 188, 189, 191
Hibon, M.   187
Holland, D.   159
Hoover, K. D.   86
Hurst, I.   164, 165
Husebø, T. A.   189

Irons, . S.   89

Jarque, C. M.   45
Jenkins, G. M.   76
Jenkinson, T.   105, 107
Jessen, H.   106, 122
Johansen, S.   29
Judd, J. P.   89
Juselius, K.   189

203

Jørgensen, C. 29

Kiviet, J. F. 45
Kongsted, H. C. 29
Krolzig, H.-M. 86, 113

Lansbury, M. L. 152
Lucas, R. E. 48, 89

Makridakis, S. 187
Marget, A. W. 34
Marquez, J. 69, 70, 87, 89
Mills, T. C. 111
Mitchell, B. R. 35
Mizon, G. E. 29, 191
Monetary Policy Committee 143
Morgan, J. 154
Morgenstern, O. 34
Morris, D. 105, 107

Nielsen, B. 29
NIESR 164
Nymoen, R. 189

Osborn, D. R. 106, 108–111, 113,
          119, 121–123
Öcal, N. 121

Pagan, A. 76
Pain, N. 24, 152, 159
Paroulo, P. 29
Perez, S. J. 86
Pesaran, M. H. 101, 103, 121
Potter, S. M. 121
Prestwich, K. M. 79

Rahbek, A. 29

Sargan, J. D. 76
Scadding, J. L. 89
Scott, A. 107, 113
Sefton, J. 152
Sensier, M. 108–111, 113, 119, 123
Simpson, P. W. 106, 108, 110, 111,
          113, 119, 122
Singer, M. 2, 19, 22, 77
Smith, J. 121
Starr, R. M. 89
Steiner, V. 154

Taylor, J. B. 48, 50

Teräsvirta, T. 112
Tran, H.-A. 29
Turner, D. S. 190

te Velde, D. 159
Vickers, J. 125, 126

Wallis, K. F. 24, 69, 74
Watson, G. S. 45
West, K. D. 89
Whitley, J. 132

Subject Index

Accuracy   10, 16, 27, 33, 43, 45, 90,
   172, 178,
   Also see Forecast
   accuracy
Aggregation   139
ARCH   45
Asymmetry   107
Autoregressive model   70

Business cycle   12, 104–106, 108,
   112, 114, 115, 122, 173

Causal information
   In forecasting   105, 111, 115,
   121, 122, 126, 187
Cointegration   30, 189,
      Also see Equilibrium
      correction
Concepts in forecasting
   Forecastable   18, 115,
      Also see Unpredictable
Conditional
   — distribution   95, 99
   — variance   96, 98
Constant term   45, 82, 190
Consumption   129, 138, 142, 151,
   156, 158

Data   20, 59, 62, 174
   — revision   174, 177
Deterministic shifts   5, 7, 22, 25,
   189, 190
Deterministic terms   21, 40, 188
Diagnostic test   45
Differencing   37, 40
Dynamic model   76, 81, 83, 87

Econometric models   6, 13, 20, 24,
   40, 56, 69, 89, 91, 98, 170,
   186, 188, 189
Economic
   — forecasting   2–4, 6, 7, 10, 16,
   17, 19, 20, 24, 41, 54, 57, 59, 63,
   68, 115, 149, 171, 173, 186
   — policy   11, 17, 20, 42, 49, 89,
   90, 107, 181
   — system   24, 171
   — theory   11, 22, 42, 43, 45, 93,
   150
Empirical model   16, 29, 48, 93, 96
Equilibrium
   — correction   156, 162
   — mean   189
Exogenous variable   45, 46, 132
Expenditure   21, 29, 82, 139, 182

Feedback   150, 165, 183
Forecast
   — accuracy   7, 11, 23, 186, 189
   — confidence interval   27, 38,
   87
   — evaluation   12, 93, 103, 169
   — failure   8, 11, 17, 20, 22, 26,
   33, 39, 89, 186, 188, 189
   — origin   33, 190
Forecast-error taxonomy   89

Gaussian   74,
      Also see Normal
      distribution
GiveWin   92
Growth rates   16, 35, 36, 110, 112,
   114, 120, 187

Histogram   30, 36

House prices   61, 137, 179, 180

Identities   46, 55
Income   12, 38, 55, 68, 69, 78, 79,
        81, 86, 129, 156
Inference   18
Inflation   7, 11, 12, 21, 28, 30, 33,
        48, 49, 51, 54, 55, 58, 60,
        64, 66, 69, 72, 81, 82, 95,
        101, 103, 107, 122, 124,
        127–129, 132, 136, 138,
        141, 142, 145, 148, 152,
        154, 160, 163, 164, 166,
        168, 173, 175, 176, 178,
        179, 181, 182, 184, 188
Information
    — set   100
    Causal —   26, 187, 190
Instrument   171
Intercept correction   190
Interest rate   12, 31, 34, 47, 50, 55,
        61, 63, 66, 82, 104, 107,
        116, 118–122, 129, 143,
        148, 158, 160, 165, 176,
        178, 181, 183

Leading indicator   12, 24, 64, 104,
        115, 120, 140
Lucas critique   89,
        Also see Econometric
        models

Mis-specification   7, 69, 77, 79,
        188,
        Also see Diagnostic test,
        Test
Model
    — mis-specification   6, 186
    — specification   22
Modeling structural change   152,
        169
Monetary system   29
Money
    — demand   146
    M1   29, 33

Monte Carlo   75, 188
MSFE   27, 75, 121

Non-linear   34, 110, 112, 114, 121
Non-stationarity   6, 11, 41, 189
    Unit roots   189
        Also see Deterministic shifts
Normal distribution   30, 36
Normality   32

Parsimonious   150
PcGive   41, 92
Prices   21, 29, 33, 47, 57, 65, 71,
        128, 132, 143, 159, 160,
        163, 168, 176, 177
Probability   12, 45, 58, 73, 75, 95,
        98, 104, 107, 113, 114,
        116, 118, 122, 132, 137,
        148

Random number   75
Random walk   82–84, 86
    — with drift   44
Rational expectations   48, 165
Residual autocorrelation   44
Restrictions   23

Selection
    Model —   110
Serial correlation   44
Simulation   29, 45, 49, 52, 89, 164,
        167, 189,
        Also see Monte Carlo
Stochastic
    — variable   21, 189
    — process   11, 16, 21, 24, 29, 33,
        35, 42–45, 52, 69, 83, 187
Structural
    — breaks   7, 16, 45, 78
    — change   13, 147, 149,
        152–154, 156, 160, 163, 165

Taxonomy of forecast errors   153
Test   32, 94
    — for normality   45

Constancy — 89
Time dependence 82, 84
Transformations 77
Trend 7, 18, 22, 37, 39, 80, 82, 83,
   166, 173, 176, 178, 188,
   189
 Linear — 21, 37, 40, 79

Unbiased expectations
 Unbiased forecast 38
Unemployment 7, 11, 54, 55, 95,
   96, 107, 144, 145, 154,
   160, 162, 164, 176
Unforecastable 19, 112,
   Also see Unpredictable
Unpredictable 18, 19, 21, 33, 188
Updating 40

Variable
 Endogenous — 45
Variance
 Forecast-error — 85
Vector autoregression (VAR) 142,
   146
Volatility 85, 166

Wages 144, 163
White noise 98

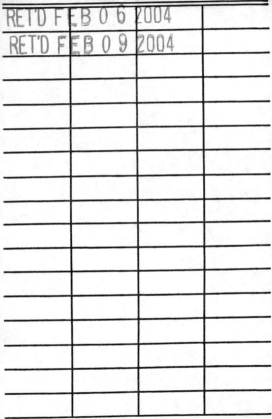

DATE DUE

RET'D FEB 0 6 2004		
RET'D FEB 0 9 2004		

DEMCO 38-297